Vasiliu

FORTY PLUS
and FANCY FREE

Books by Emily Kimbrough

OUR HEARTS WERE YOUNG AND GAY (with Cornelia Otis Skinner)
WE FOLLOWED OUR HEARTS TO HOLLYWOOD
HOW DEAR TO MY HEART
IT GIVES ME GREAT PLEASURE . . .
THE INNOCENTS FROM INDIANA
THROUGH CHARLEY'S DOOR
FORTY PLUS AND FANCY FREE

FORTY
PLUS
and FANCY FREE

by EMILY KIMBROUGH

Drawings by MIRCEA VASILIU

HARPER & BROTHERS · PUBLISHERS · NEW YORK

To Margie, Marian, Sophy and Zella
who made the trip and, therefore, the book.
With love

FORTY PLUS
and FANCY FREE

Chapter 1

I CAN'T GO to Italy," I said one morning last March, "without knowing something of the language." I made this pronouncement in a loud voice. The apartment was empty, there was no one to hear me. But I have my idiosyncrasy like the bellman in *The Snark*, who maintained, "What I say three times is true."

My idiosyncrasy is that what I say out loud is likely to come true. Therefore, I do not say aloud other plans for the future I frequently think about; studying to be an opera singer, being selected by Mr. Astaire or Mr. Kelly as a dancing partner in an M.G.M. extravaganza, or giving Katherine Cornell a run for her money.

But when on the fifteenth of March, I said aloud that I ought to learn some Italian before going to Italy, I knew at that instant I was probably going to Italy.

An hour earlier I had listened to considerable promotional talk from my friend, Sophy, who lives in Philadelphia but shares my apartment when she is in New York. Sophy is a very busy woman. She is Vice-President of the National Urban League and an active participant in several other organizations. She is a vigorous campaigner and a great one for planning. Her hair is curly and has been gray since she was thirty-five. When she brings it on end by running her hands through it and says, "Now darling . . ." you

1

know you're involved in a campaign and a plan, and it's a ninety to one bet that, as of that minute, you're a goner.

"Italy," she had urged, "I haven't been to Italy since 1927, and you've never been there at all except a few days in Venice twenty-five years ago. That scarcely counts. Then we would fly to England for the Coronation. I think it's better to make England the end of the trip instead of the beginning, because by June, Italy will be too hot."

All this had sounded reasonable, except for including me in it. I have been to Europe a number of times, many of my friends have gone abroad more than once, some even with regularity. And yet I have never outgrown the astonishment I felt at the age of twelve when a contemporary of mine in Muncie, Indiana, Emily Shirk, was taken by her family to Egypt and came back with picture postcards of the trip. Perhaps this astonishment is due to my childhood conditioning. To go anywhere from Indiana was a considerable undertaking.

Traveling on lecture tours the last number of years has not filled in these grooves of memory, because the tours have not been of my deciding. My itinerary is sent to me and tickets placed in my hand. A self-propelled trip is a very different matter.

I have a friend who understands this point of view and shares it, but not from the same background. Kitty Cassard, a Philadelphian by birth and unchanged environment, is, of course, conservative. When a trip is proposed to her, her invariable response is, "I'd like to go, but I have to think first how it would be."

I have to think back all the way to the depot in Indianapolis and take a running start from there. I was running when I said I thought I'd better learn Italian.

As unselective as a mountain stream on its way to the sea, I was picking up things as I went along; maps of all the countries in Europe, including the Scandinavian, a new travel book on Italy by Sydney Clark called *All the Best in Italy*, and I caught up a friend I happened to be passing.

Margie, who is Sophy's sister, came over from Philadelphia where she lives, to spend the night in New York at my apartment. Margie and Sophy look startlingly alike, except that Margie, though older, still has by nature, blond hair. Temperamentally there is very little resemblance. Margie dislikes organizations, campaigns, and plans. Foreknowledge of any expedition is to her synonymous with curtailment of liberty. She shies from an engagement calendar like a nervous horse at the sight of a scrap of paper.

I showed my accumulation to her. "I'm gathering up whatever I can," I told her, and had an idea. "Why don't you come, too?" I asked.

She shied from my suggestion. She couldn't possibly do such a thing, she insisted. She had children and grandchildren. They might need her. She had flown once in 1937 from London to Paris and was certainly not going to do it again. She had never in her life traveled with a group of women. She wasn't at all sure she'd care for it. She was prancing about my living room as she talked, waving the long cigarette holder she always uses, taking quick puffs, blowing the smoke out breathlessly.

I flouted all her objections. "Two is not a group," I pointed out to her, "especially when one of them is your own sister. We haven't a husband among us so we'll just have to do without. Even in this day and age it might cause talk if you were to travel about with men, so you might try women. Don't fly, if you don't want to. Start earlier than we, go by boat and meet us in Italy. As for children, we've all got them."

When Margie mentioned her six grandchildren, I knew she was weakening. I challenged her to deny that her six put her in a more exalted rank than Sophy's with five, and mine with one, beautiful remarkable, intelligent grandson.

"We're all grandmothers," I reiterated, "and if anything happens to any of our grandchildren there's nothing we can do about it anyway. Our young don't need us and the sooner we face up to that the better off everybody will be. You know that as well as I do," I wound up. "You're just in the Indianapolis depot. That's what's holding you back."

I suppose Margie knows there is such a place as Indianapolis, but to find herself there is beyond the farthest stretch of her imagination, I'm sure. The very idea of such an imprisonment sent her scuttling in the opposite direction.

"I'll go to Europe with you," she said.

Sophy, the next day learning I had gathered up Margie, was amazed but pleased. "I wouldn't have thought of it myself," she said, "and I don't know how in the world you persuaded her, but I think it's fine. Have you anyone else in mind?"

"I hadn't had Margie in mind," I admitted, but I was pleased to accept the credit for having annexed her.

The next few days I didn't see any friends. I was preoccupied with the matter of presenting in the best possible light to my employers, the Columbia Broadcasting Company, my proposed trip. I had been in the employ of this company only for seven months, giving a daily radio program. And it had been so many years since I had worked for an organization I had failed to include in my calculations for the trip the necessity of receiving permission to make it. Delivering aloud an announcement is an abracadabra that works for *me*, I realized, in these hours of preoccupation, but it might not be a sufficiently powerful magic to bring an entire organization to heel.

Unable to conjure up a better way of dealing with the problem, however, I went in to the office of my boss, Mr. Sam Slate, head of radio programs, and said in a voice that lacked the firmness I had employed in my solo speech at my apartment, "Sam," I said, "I would like to go to Italy and then to England for the Coronation. I'd be gone four weeks. Do you think that would be possible?"

In my mind I was telling Margie and Sophy that the party was off so far as I was concerned due to an oversight on my part of Columbia Broadcasting.

Sam Slate is from the South. He speaks slowly and smokes

cigars. Before speaking at all he has to make comfortable adjustment of the cigar. I therefore had plenty of time to undo the entire
trip before I heard him say, "We'd like to have you broadcast the
Coronation. Suppose you broadcast two weeks from London, and
take the two weeks in Italy as your vacation."

I felt as if walking up a flight of stairs I had climbed a top step
that wasn't there. The resultant jar dimmed Sam's further remarks
that had something to do with making contact with the British
Broadcasting Corporation (BBC) to secure a time and a circuit,
and various other technicalities that even in the best of health I
would not have understood. I left his office, however, with the
groggy impression that I could resume my course to the sea.

That night I picked up Zella. Our friendship dates from college
days, and that is a date we do not care to mention. She and her
husband dropped in from Lyme, Connecticut, where they live.
Zella has black hair and eyes and the temperament that frequently
accompanies these attributes. She moves quickly, physically and
mentally.

Within an hour of their arrival, she was added to the party, with
her husband's enthusiastic corroboration of her decision. We now
made four. Since we had no other visitors that evening we were
still at four the next morning when Lady Moray, an old friend of
Sophy's, telephoned that she was in New York, had flown over
from London where she lives, and would like to see Sophy.

Returning that afternoon from my broadcast, I found them
together in my apartment.

Sophy broke in on my greeting. "Barbara," she said, "has offered
us her house in London for the two weeks we are there, even
including three maids."

I hope Barbara interpreted my babbling response as an expression
of gratitude.

Sophy chimed in. "The house, and the apartment in the mews
behind will sleep four, five at a stretch. I thought you ought to
know that and remember it," she added darkly.

There was not the faintest possibility of our numbering more than four, I told Sophy, and turned away from her to reiterate to Barbara how overwhelmed I was by her generosity, and how delightful it would be to have a house of our own as base, instead of whatever rooms we could get on the outskirts of London. I'd been told all hotels in London were already booked solid.

Barbara explained that because of requests from the countries of the Commonwealth for larger representation in the Abbey than had hitherto been granted them, new rules had been made that would lessen the British representation there. One of these rules was that widows of peers would not be invited. Since Barbara's husband had died a few years ago, she came under this category. And that, she explained, was why she had decided to leave the crowds of London, go to the country, and in peace and quiet watch the ceremony on television. Arabella, the youngest of her three daughters, wanted to stay in London, but at the house of one of her married sisters, so they might share the fun and the gaiety of the parties that would lead up to and follow the Coronation itself.

We were back to the beginning again.

"So you see," Barbara said, "I don't want the house, and I'd like you to have it."

After she had gone, Sophy and I let ourselves drift into dreamy contemplation of how it would be. We would give little dinner parties, gay but select. People would come for tea. There would be suppers after the theater. The last fantasy was my proposal, due to my having read about early curtain time at the theater in London, and the habit of dining afterward that has grown up as a consequence.

Sophy returned to Philadelphia, but was back again in a few days, a little subdued, I thought.

Taking up where we had left off at her departure, our idyl of entertaining in London, I was interrupted by Sophy.

"I told all this to Margie," she said, "and she was thrilled about the house. But do you know what she said about the entertaining? She said, 'It sounds perfectly wonderful. Do you know anybody in London?' "

This was a surprising thought to me, as evidently it had been to Sophy. Reviewing hastily in my mind the entire area of London, I came to the dismal realization that in all of it I knew not one human being.

Sophy made an additional contribution to the London picture. "There are going to be five of us. Marian Boyer is going to fly over just for the Coronation. There's one more bed in the house. If we give it to her she promises to get seats for us. Of course that really doesn't concern you," she added pointedly.

This was true. I was sitting pretty, I had already been told, by courtesy of BBC.

I told Sophy hastily I was delighted to have Marian. And I was. She would be fun, I knew, and is an old friend.

Sophy interrupted, "What difference does it make whether we're four or five women, anyway, as long as we've found out we don't know anybody in London. It's a sorry picture. A lovely house, crawling with women and three maids, and not a soul coming in from the outside."

We pictured this moodily, until remembering I, too, had not been idle during Sophy's absence, I broke into the silence. "I'm signing up at the Berlitz School," was my announcement, "for Italian lessons." I repeated the dictum that had boosted me into the trip. "You can't go to Italy without knowing something of the language."

Sophy pondered this. "I'll join you," she volunteered unenthusiastically. She was obviously still moping over the London isolation period ahead. "I won't be so good as you," she admitted, "because you've got a much better musical ear than I have, though I know more about music than you do," she inserted. "However, I'll try not to hold you back."

I was magnanimous. She wouldn't hold me back at all, I promised, and I'd be glad of her company.

She asked if I'd ever gone to the Berlitz School. I hadn't, but my daughter, B, had studied French there one winter.

"That was the year she went to Sarah Lawrence," I explained. "They couldn't take her until the second semester, so she took French all fall at the Berlitz."

I was engulfed suddenly by a happy prospect, and beamed. "She didn't get in all the lessons, but I paid for the course. That was five years ago, but I don't see why the credit isn't still good. It's worth trying."

There are few things more stimulating to me than the incentive of a bargain; not paying at all is intoxication. I jumped for the telephone.

"Any time tomorrow morning," I reported to Sophy at the end of my conversation, "to discuss arrangements. Do you think she'll understand about B and my credit? She speaks with an accent."

"That doesn't surprise me at the Berlitz School," Sophy said, "but I've a hunch you'll get the idea through to her."

Chapter 2

THE FOLLOWING morning, Sophy and I, around nine-thirty, enrolled in the Berlitz School. The address was Rockefeller Center, that part of it with an entrance on Fifth Avenue. Immediately inside this entrance we confronted a double flight of escalators, one going up and directly beside it the descending flight. Sophy was all for boarding the upgoing one. When I asked for what purpose, her answer was that there didn't seem to be anything at the bottom. I pointed out to her a characteristic I have noticed during the twenty-five years we've been friends. This is a habit of keeping in motion when endeavoring to reach an unfamiliar destination. I, on the other hand, I pointed out, holding her at the foot of the escalator, like to pause to get my bearing, either by looking around or by inquiring. When I have gone with her on a motor trip, I have occasionally persuaded her to ask directions of an attendant at a gas station, but I have yet to see her wait for his answer.

Sophy's response to this impromptu character reading was a concession. She would forego climbing the stairs, she said, if I would bring her anyone of whom we might ask directions. With all the bustle we had just left on Fifth Avenue, there was, curiously, not a soul in this large, dark foyer. I released my grip on her arm in order to look for someone, and she immediately started up the steps. I walked to the right of the stairway and almost at once came upon a large show window containing a display of the workings of the Berlitz School. A cardboard figure of a stylish gentleman dwarf dominated the scene. He wore a morning coat, gray trousers, his collar was exceptionally high. I thought he was a dwarf because the size of his head made the rest of him seem of diminutive proportions. But perhaps this ratio was intended only to convey an outsize intellect. This was further indicated by an extra large pair of black, horn-rimmed spectacles and total lack of hair on his head. The figure carried a long pointer of the sort teachers use at a blackboard. This was directed to a cardboard sign listing a series of languages headed by French. Along the floor at the foot of the figure, a row of books emphasized the intellectual tone of the scene. Each bore the over-all title, *The Berlitz Self Teacher*, and below it the language that particular volume would impart. Another cardboard sign near by read, "ENROLL TODAY." It was only after I had studied at some length the awesome prospect behind this invitation, that I came upon, in small type, the information that the School itself was on the fifth floor.

There was no possibility of sharing with Sophy this discovery. She had long since passed beyond my view.

I did not know how to reach the fifth floor, since the escalator in the center seemed to end within sight directly above me. Several people came in from the street. I asked one of these if he knew where the elevators were. He directed me to their hiding place behind the escalator.

When I left the conveyance at the fifth floor, I saw almost at once a metal sign pointing in the direction of the School, and labeled. I therefore did not have to ask directions again.

The first person I saw as I came through the door was Sophy, standing at a long counter, her back to me. She was talking to a young woman on the other side of the counter. I joined Sophy.

"We're together," I told the young woman.

Sophy turned. "Oh, I'm glad you got here," she said. "Find some-one to tell you the way?"

I continued to the young woman. "My daughter," I told her —I said each word slowly and distinctly in order not to confuse her with rapid English—"took a course in French from your school, but she didn't finish it. We lived in Philadelphia then, and this was five years ago. Do you think the credit could be trans-ferred—unless there is a time limit on it? Perhaps you don't under-stand what I'm saying, but if you will let me speak to the manager here, I'm sure I could—"

Miss Berlitz interrupted me. She was small, dark, had brown eyes and a patient smile. "There will be no trouble about the credit," she said briskly, and her accent was as Middle Western as mine, "as long as you get permission from your daughter."

I stared at her. Sophy made a disagreeable sound, very like a snicker.

"Why," I said incredulously, "I don't believe you do understand. *I* paid for the course. I'm her mother."

My vis-à-vis was patient.

"It was your daughter who went to the classes. *She* registered. Therefore, it's for her to say whether at some time she wishes to continue the lessons and complete the course, or transfer to you those remaining. If you will give me her name and address, I'll have our office write to her asking for a release to you."

"She's gone to California with her baby on a month's visit to my parents," I reported. "She's been married since she took that course."

Sophy broke in. "I don't believe the Berlitz School is getting up a dossier on B," she told me. "Just your family's address will do."

I delivered the address and the young woman wrote it down. She then took my registration; Sophy's, I found, had already been taken care of. We were to have a lesson every morning, sharing a teacher, but with no one else in the class.

"You may start now, if you wish," our registrar said, and gathered up the papers we had signed. "Classroom L."

As we walked down the hall in the direction she had indicated, I admitted my irritation. "It's silly," I said, "but I'm irked by such nonsense. What on earth has B got to do with *my* Italian? I paid for her lessons and she was too lazy to finish them. Now *she* gives *me* permission to take Italian. What I really mind is that she's going to think it's very, very funny. It's almost put me off the whole idea."

Sophy asked if I'd feel better just to pay for my lessons and forget the credit. Obviously this was nonsense; I said nothing more.

There was considerable traffic up and down the corridor, men and women, young girls and boys, most of them carrying notebooks, textbooks, pencils. I had a sudden wistful fantasy that I was back at college again, and wondered how it would be if I stopped some of these people to ask if they had seen the Dean to arrange their courses and what were the professors like. But such snatches of conversation as I overheard were in foreign languages, no two of them the same and not one of them English. I felt suddenly shy and scuttled after Sophy, who as usual was ahead of me. She turned into a room on the left, stopping to look at the letter on the door. I followed her across the threshold and there I was, in a classroom like classrooms the world over, except that this was smaller than most. Three rows of chairs, each with a wide arm on which to put books and notebook for writing, a desk by the door where the professor would sit. The room, at the moment, was empty. Sophy was standing still, looking around her, like me.

"It takes me back thirty years," I said. "I feel kind of queer."

Sophy nodded.

We took off our coats and gloves, and piled them on chairs in the back row. We selected places on the front row and sat down side by side, though there was plenty of space in which to spread ourselves more comfortably. Neither of us seemed to find anything more to say to the other.

On the threshold I had noticed vaguely that the walls were hung with pictures. I took more careful note of them while we waited for the professor, or whatever was going to happen next. And of all the storytelling pictures I have ever seen, these held the record for content.

The one on the wall directly in front of me included, looking from left down around the border and up to the right-hand corner, a ferry boat on a blue ocean, a group of people on a beach, the ladies dressed in suits of the Annette Kellerman period, a hooded wicker bath chair. Next, the skyline of New York, a dirigible floating overhead, a four-masted schooner in the harbor, an ocean liner with a tug pulling it and a hydroplane settling down just alongside. A bathroom came next, with tub and basin, soap, sponge, comb, pair of scissors, tube of toothpaste.

By this time I had realized that the purpose of these pictures was for us to learn the name of each of the objects contained in whatever language we were studying. It occurred to me that if this were the objective, it was a badly timed sense of delicacy that excluded the one object in a bathroom for which one undoubtedly would have the most urgent need in the language of the country one was visiting.

A bedroom scene balanced the bathroom; very quaint, with a ruffled canopy over the bed and around the dressing table. I made a mental note that I would not tax my intellectual capacity with the Italian for ruffles.

I had not, as yet, come to the borders. When I reached my scrutiny of these I knew at once that Mr. Berlitz was going to ask more of me than I would be able to give him. Down the left border, in order, were a squirrel, a peacock, a frog, a duck, a beetle and a pair of duelists matching swords. Across the bottom a bee, a boiled egg in a cup, a pig, a cheese under glass, a glass of beer—that was all to the good—two roosters, a patch of mushrooms, an artist sitting at an easel; next, a roll of sausage, a loaf of bread, and cantering up the opposite side, an ostrich followed by a swan, a caterpillar, a butterfly, an owl, a typewriter, a telephone, a stork, a parrot, an eagle, three fish, of to me unknown species, and a large wolf in a snowdrift.

I turned to Sophy for the purpose of telling her I intended to take a stand on how wide an area I wished my Italian to cover, when a voice from the doorway said, *"Buon giorno."*

I turned with a start to see, bowing gracefully at us from the doorway, a handsome young man, obviously Italian, with black hair in a waving pompadour and large brown eyes.

Out of the corner of my eye I saw Sophy, rather red in the face, give a stiff little nod. I heard her mutter, but I doubt that it reached the young man, *"Buon giorno."*

I tried to make my acknowledgment somewhere between Sophy's nod and the young man's bow. I found myself unable, because I felt silly, to produce a *"Buon giorno,"* but I gave out something in the nature of a whinny with a smile.

The young man seated himself at the desk by the door. He was carrying a book and two quite large white cards. He pushed these on top of the desk, bent over, looked at the cards, picked up one of them and looking from it to each of us in turn said inquiringly, "Signora Kimbrough?"

"Moi," I answered loudly as if faulty hearing on his part was the stumbling block between us, and I pointed to my chest. With the instant realization, however, that my remark did not sound Italian, I added stiffly, "I am Mrs. Kimbrough."

The young man shook his head and pointed to me. *"Lei è Signora Kimbrough."* He put the palm of his hand against his chest. *"Io sono Signor Grammatico."* He repeated this back and forth several times, and then turned to Sophy.

"Signora Jacobs?" he inquired.

"Io sono Signora Jacobs," Sophy replied.

"Bravo, bravo," said Signor Grammatico, and they smiled at each other.

I had a deplorable impulse to give her a swift kick in the ankle.

Signor Grammatico picked up his book. "*Il libro*," he said pointing to it. "*Il lapis*," he picked up the pencil; "*la tavola*," he patted
the table; "*la penna*," he showed us his fountain pen; "*la sedia*,"
and he bounced to indicate that was what he was sitting on; "*il
muro*," he indicated the wall, "*il soffitto*," and pointed to the
ceiling.

He lifted the book and looked inquiringly at me. "*Que è?*" he
said with a rousing inflection and I gathered he wanted me to tell
him what it was.

"*Le libro*," I answered, and tried not to sound smug.

He shook his head. "*Il libro*," he corrected me.

We went on to the other objects. I gave these back to him in
Italian and I made only one other error. I confused "chair" with
"ceiling." "*La soffito*," I said, and bounced in my concentration on
doing exactly what he had done.

"*Il soffitto*," he corrected, and pointed upward. "*La sedia*," and
indicated where I had bounced.

I had already regretted the bouncing and was doubly mortified
it had taken place on "the ceiling."

He turned to Sophy.

Sophy rattled off the objects with the rapidity of a chattering
squirrel, and ending up with "*il libro*," drew out the vowel and
gave the *r* the kind of roll Caruso used to send out into the auditorium from the stage of the Metropolitan. My delivery had been
uncompromisingly Muncie, Indiana.

I slewed around in my chair and stared at my companion. She
was leaning forward smiling, her head at a coquettish tilt, her
cheeks flushed, her eyes sparkling and fixed on Signor Grammatico.

"*Bravissimo*." I heard Signor Grammatico murmur, and I resumed my former position facing him. Not that he was aware
which way I was facing. He and Sophy were exchanging staccato
nods of mutual congratulation.

There is an old hymn that begins, "I am a stranger here." The second line continues, "Heaven is my home." This latter I waved aside as not applicable. But for the first line, spiritually speaking, the writer of that hymn and I were in precisely the same spot.

The lingual tour of the room continued. Signora Jacobs and Signor Grammatico led the way, the rolling *r*'s cascading behind them. I tagged along like an unwanted kid sister they'd been told to look out for. Sometimes the Signor tossed an inquiry at me, and Sophy would repeat the word to me helpfully, much in the way adults ask a child learning the rudiments of speech, "Where is baby's nose?" says one, and the other echoes, "Nose, darling?" But Baby Kimbrough was by this time too addled to respond. In the end Signor Grammatico and Sophy evidently decided it was kinder to leave me alone. And so while I sat muttering to myself the two or three words I had managed to capture early in the hour, they trilled their *r*'s and glided their vowels, from pocketbook to handkerchief to dress, suit, hat, shoes and so on.

A bell ringing was the first familiar sound I heard in sixty minutes. I knew what it meant, too, and that in itself was a comfort. It meant the class was over and I was mercifully released. The bell was a surprise to Sophy and Signor Grammatico. They stopped the rondo on which they were engaged and shook their heads in a spontaneous expression of disappointment that such a pleasant hour had sped away. I was already at the chair in the back of the room where I had placed my coat and gloves. For fifty-five minutes I had been far, far in the rear. But sixty minutes and thirty seconds from the time I had entered that room found me going out of it, coated and gloved.

"*Arrivederci*," or some such nonsense Signor Grammatico called after me. But I was safely across the threshold.

"Good-bye," I said.

Passing the main desk in the entrance hall, I was hailed by the girl who had taken my registration, the same one who was going to ask my daughter's permission for me to be taught Italian on credit. I was in no mood for any further trafficking with the young woman

and would have gone on my way but she called after me. "I think
you will want to buy a book. They're on sale here."

I approached her and her book cautiously. I was not prepared
to say whether or not I wanted a book, because I was not sure
that my brief association with the Berlitzes and their doings was
going to continue. The young woman, however, held out invitingly
to me a slim volume and I took it. Sophy joined me while I was
examining it and immediately asked for one for herself.

On the way to the elevator she prattled about how exhilarating
the hour had been, how her rusty old brain had come alive again,
making her realize how much she had always loved languages.
Once we were out on Fifth Avenue, I parted from her and her
exhilaration. I did not see her again until evening.

By that time, however, I had made up my mind to go on with
Mr. Berlitz and Signor Grammatico and all the rest of them, because I had said that one shouldn't go to Italy without knowing
something of the language. This was what had really started me
on the trip and I had better keep going, if one could call what I
had accomplished in Italian to date "going" anywhere.

Sophy was spending the weekdays in New York at my apartment, returning to her own house in Haverford for the week ends.
She had volunteered to plan with the travel agency our itinerary
in Italy, see about renting a car, and the rest of us had gratefully en-
dorsed her offer.

I would not for the world take anything from her generosity,
but unselfish as she is, I cannot help feeling that certain other
factors may have contributed to her inherent thoughtfulness. One,
that Zella, competent as she is, lives in Lyme. To consult with
New York travel agencies would therefore not be very convenient.
Two, that Margie, Sophy's sister, has never in her life planned a
trip and is by nature reluctant to make a decision of no greater
magnitude than how and when to go to Philadelphia from her
own house in suburban Chestnut Hill. And finally, that I am unable to read a map.

Therefore, Sophy was very busy and I did not see her during the daytime. The evening of my stumble into Italian, however, she was at the apartment poring over her map. I wanted to pore over the Italian book that had been put into my hand by the registration clerk but I was embarrassed. I waited until she had gone to her room and I was safely in my bed before I turned its pages. My dogged purpose, if it took me all night, was to catch up to where Sophy and Signor Grammatico had rested at the ringing of the bell.

At intervals during the day I had looked forward to this catching up. It would be like cramming for an exam, I had pictured. Many was the night, I had reminded myself, I had put a wet towel around my head and studied right through until the dawn pausing only for an occasional cup of strong, black coffee. I drink Sanka now, and that, I thought, would be the only difference. I leaned back happily against my pillow and opened to page one.

I had no need of a wet towel to help me. I had no need of the book itself, certainly no use from it, because it contained not one single word of English; just a listing of the words I had supposedly learned in my "*lezione primo*." I could read the words but of what good was that to me when I had no means of telling a "*scapola*" from a "*denaro*."

Before I went to sleep, however, I could say every word on the list of the "*lezione primo*" like a parrot. The only ones I could pick out at random were "*porta*," "*finestra*" and "*libro*," because they were the only ones to which I could attach a meaning. But I had the complete list down pat so long as it remained in sequence.

I tried them over the next morning the minute I awakened, and was pleased to find I still could rattle them off, though I was not yet up to drawn-out vowels and rolling *r*'s.

On our way to the school I said nothing to Sophy about my last night's accomplishment. I intended it to be a surprise.

We had a new teacher that morning, a gentleman, but not so dashing as Signor Grammatico; his was a steam roller model. We

moved slowly but inexorably into counting and numbers. There
was no foolish skittering around over the ground we had covered
the day before. Not once was I given opportunity to recite my
word poem made up from the *"lezione primo."* Counting from
one to one hundred was our route for the day, and I was fine up
to five. Five in Italian is spelled *"cinque"* and pronounced "chin-
que." Since five in French is spelled *"cinq"* and pronounced
"sank," I gave that pronunciation to *"cinque."* I was corrected.
The next time round I said "sank-que." I was corrected. The following time I gave "chank-que."

This evidence of imbecility was doubly exasperating to me
because for a long time I have thought, and even said to anyone
who might be interested, that I get by far a greater number of
impressions by ear than I do by sight. I pick up music fairly easily.
I even play by ear. The execution is bad but I render the tune
accurately.

All these things I said to myself with fury while Sophy flashed
from one to one hundred.

Starting with six, I was what I please to call a humdinger until
we reached fifteen. Fifteen is spelled *"quindici"* and pronounced as
in "quince." I accepted that and returned it with no difficulty,
and we moved on to twenty. But at twenty we stopped and went
back to one, and at five I was at the old standstill again; "sank,"
"sank-que," "chank-que," and now added to it a possible "chin-
dici," et cetera.

The professor was kindness and patience itself. Sophy was kind
and patient, too. I would have given anything to return to the
spirit of indifference to me that, due to the *rapprochement* between Sophy and Signor Grammatico, had prevailed the preceding
day.

When the bell rang I was in the eighties, but still wobbly at
any number with a five in it. I stopped at the sound of the bell.
The professor put up his hand arresting my motion of getting up
to leave. He rose from his desk, walked over to my chair and bent

over me, first giving a furtive look over his shoulder toward the door. "You're going to Italy, aren't you?" he asked in a little more than a whisper.

The sound of my own tongue delivered in this conspiratorial fashion so startled me I drew back and could only nod in reply.

"Well, then," and his voice strengthened a little with urgency, "get those fives. You don't want to be gypped, do you?"

I thanked him in a whisper for his concern.

Each day following brought a new teacher, except for a repeat with Signor Grammatico. Sophy gave him a dazzling performance, to which he responded with enough "*bravos*" to fill up a page in Mr. Berlitz's *libro Italiano*. They even exchanged sallies of wit. I suppose that is what they were because of the mutual happy laughter each sentence brought. I would not have been surprised to see the Signor and the Signora push back the chairs and treat themselves to a little waltz turn.

On the last day of the course we had a lady teacher. She was somewhat elderly, rather frail, and was catching a cold. She wore a shawl around her shoulders and in addition to the inevitable book and cards, carried a box of Kleenex. Evidently the cards produced on the first day were handed to each succeeding teacher, because I could see them gradually being filled, the professor of each day adding to the contents left by his predecessors. Some wrote more than others. Signor Grammatico's notes, I had noticed, were brief, but the Signora of our last day wrote fully after each recitation she drew from one or the other of us. Between times she used a Kleenex apologetically.

We were into sentences now, she posing a question to each and eliciting a fully phrased response. At least that was her intention and it was fulfilled by one of us. She worked hard and earnestly; she was an excellent teacher. When the bell rang she was writing on one of the cards. At the sound she looked up "*Molto bene,*" she said to Sophy, "*molto, molto bene.*"

She took a fresh Kleenex from the box, held it to her nose and turned to me. "*Coraggio, Signora,*" she said, "*coraggio e avanti.*"

"That means 'courage,'" Sophy said, " 'courage and keep going.' "

Chapter 3

O N SATURDAY afternoon at five o'clock on May 2, Sophy, Zella and I left Idlewild on a plane bound for Paris. Margie had sailed two days before. She would land in Naples and join us in Rome. She had not been persuaded to fly with us, though she was not happy about the transportation she had chosen. She saw herself, she told us several times before she left, arriving breathless with all her luggage piled around her at one hotel after another throughout Italy, and being met on the doorstep of each hostelry by its proprietor who would point urgently toward the distance and say, "They left this morning. They said tell you their next stop would be . . ." and he would name some one of the hill towns plotted on our itinerary. The reiterated assurances on our part that we would wait did not change her mournful foresight.

Neither Sophy, Zella nor I went to the pier to see her off. We were too busy with our own last-minute urgencies. It was just as well. We were spared, until we met in Rome, the knowledge of the amount of luggage she carried. Her children came with her from Philadelphia to see her on her way and reported later to Sophy that she had actually put out to sea. During the two days preceding her departure she had, by telephone, communicated to Sophy every few hours her intention of giving up the whole trip.

The three of us, Sophy, Zella and I, collected a considerable group to speed our departure; children, in-laws, grandchildren, one husband, Zella's; one parent, Zella's. It totaled eleven. Before a smaller audience I might have gone one step farther than Margie. Not *said* I was going to call off the trip, but called it off and taken a taxi back to town.

I was deterred from heading for home by the bulk of our group I would have had to butt my way through and, in lesser degree, by the grudging admission to myself that I was responsible for our having to fly. I was the one who, because of a job, could only take five weeks off. And I was the one who, somewhat quixotically, though the reasons at the time had seemed to me sound, had persuaded the others to advance by a week our date of departure. This had not been easy to accomplish, and I had had no part in its accomplishment. Sophy had done it all with long distance help from Zella, who had received with spectacular equanimity the news of my proposed change and provided an introduction to Mr. Henry Ayer. Mr. Ayer owns a travel agency and specializes in air travel. Without his help we could not have changed dates.

Taking all these things into consideration as I did at the airport, I decided to board the plane when the time came.

The reason I had yearned to bolt is that I do not like to fly. I don't count it a more luxurious way to travel than transportation in a bus or a trolley. To sit beside a passenger who may fall asleep with his mouth open and his head on my shoulder is no treat. He, however, need have no fear that his shoulder will pillow my head. I dare not allow myself a moment of relaxation, let alone sleep. The pilots may not be aware of it but I am helping them every mile of the way. My ear is sharpened to the sound of the motors; any deviation from perfect synchronization can not escape my notice. Several times an hour I fasten my eyes as unblinkingly as nature will permit on the motors, in case of oil leakage. On former flights I have tried conversation with my seatmate, but this had proved unsatisfactory. I find that I am even more uneasy if distracted from my vigil. Conversation also affects my breathing.

I am a light breather on a plane. I do not do this deliberately, but I seem unable to overcome it. I am not so half-witted as to believe that this form of breathing lessens my weight and therefore helps keep the plane up, but I have a sneaking hope that it might. A sleeping pill would make me a very different kind of passenger, I know. But I am unable to accept this panacea because I do not know how to find out, and still be considered on the safe side of lunacy, if a fellow passenger would stand watch in my place.

Zella was my seatmate. I told her as we settled in I was not an enthusiastic air traveler; this was something less than an exaggeration. I also told her I was a quiet one. She admitted later she had not anticipated my being a boisterous traveler, and was somewhat surprised to have me assure her I would be quiet. Neither, she said, had she anticipated my carrying quiet to the length of making that assurance my first and last utterance, and dedicating the entire seventeen hours of the crossing to solving in sequence an omnibus of Double-Crostics, varying this occupation only by periods of staring out the window. I protested that I hadn't done these things while eating dinner. Her answer to that was I hadn't talked either.

Sophy's seat was up the aisle so she and Zella were out of communication range. I had begged to be allowed to sit by myself, but Sophy and Zella had said, smiling indulgently, they could see I was a little nervous and thought it would be reassuring to be beside a friend. I have yet to find anyone who understands that mortal reassurance makes not the slightest difference to me.

The flight was probably charted in the log as uneventful. All the engines stopped simultaneously somewhere over the Atlantic for what seemed to me the span of a lifetime, but they did resume action again and perhaps the pilot was merely shifting gears; I prefer not to know. Around one o'clock Sunday afternoon the wheels touched ground. The trip was over. We were alive and we were almost in Paris, at Orly Airport.

At the customs house we stood at long counters that formed a

hollow square. Into the center of this ran a chute that spat out
the bags brought from the plane. As each bag descended a passenger recognizing it would call out that it was his, and one of
the group of porters standing at the bottom of the chute would
hoist it onto the counter in front of its owner. When an owner
had gathered in front of him all his luggage, he would call out,
"*complet, complet.*" This brought a customs official to attention;
he would inspect the baggage and then release it and the traveler.

In spite of the over-all confusion and noise it did not take me
long to understand this procedure and be ready to take part in it,
but my bags were an unconscionable time in arriving. Other people stepped to the counter, looked up the chute, cried out happily at the sight of a valise descending and in no time at all were
shouting that they were "complete," and receiving attention. I
saw Zella and Sophy across from me and far down the counter
gather in their treasures, summon a customs man, and still I
waited. I called out my apologies to them when I saw them waiting for me on the free side of the barrier. I knew they were as
fretful as I because Paris was so close and we had so little time.

If there was an American woman abroad whose *pièce de résist-
ance* was not a plaid carryall with hangers inside, I did not
encounter her. I was to learn on the trip that every fellow coun-
trywoman who took plane, train, or entered a hotel with me, had
with her that piece of luggage. But in my simplicity, I assumed
at the Orly customs that each plaid carryall was mine and I
shouted for it accordingly. The continuous straightening out of
this entanglement may have brought on myself and others the
delay under which I was suffering. But when finally my own, my
very own bag was on the counter in front of me, and following it
the lesser pieces, I called in French and in excited triumph, louder
than all the rest, "I am full. Here is my luggage and I am full."

The effect of this was instantaneous and gratifying. Two customs officials, not one, leaped forward instantly. One checked my
passport, the other chalked my luggage with not so much as an

inquiry as to what I might be bringing. Both of them called for porters, and they in turn came at once on the lope. This, I thought with considerable pleasure, was the result of a look at my passport. I had been identified as a member of the Columbia Broadcasting organization, and that fine company had no doubt sent word ahead that I was to be particularly looked out for.

Joining Zella and Sophy I murmured, "Did you ever see such attention? That's CBS for you, and isn't it handy?"

They agreed it was, but as we walked on toward the taxi stand outside, Sophy said it seemed queer to her that if CBS had asked them to give me all that service, they hadn't started it a little earlier, and not kept her and Zella waiting so long.

After the bags were settled in place I was assisted into the taxi by both porters. Sophy and Zella got in by themselves. The porters waited until I was seated and then leaned in the window, one on either side. "*Bon voyage*," they said to me with beaming smiles, "and felicitations."

The felicitations confused me a little and I mused over it as we drove away from the Field. An uneasy memory nagged the back of my mind, and as the taxi turned toward Paris the memory came to the front. It was of an evening in Paris in 1949 when an American friend of mine married to a Frenchman had confided to me, "I made the most awful gaff last night at a family dinner. None of them spoke English but I was doing all right in French until they urged me to take a second helping. I didn't want to hurt their feelings so I said it was perfectly delicious but that I was full." My friend had turned to me then, her eyes wide. "Do you know what it means in French if you say 'I am full'?"

I had told her I didn't know.

"Well," was her answer, "it means in coarse slang, 'I am pregnant.'"

That was what I had shouted at the counter in the customs house. That, and not CBS, was the source of the remarkable service given me. I did not share this revelation with Sophy and Zella.

The drive into Paris from Orly is long, but I was not impatient because we were moving into Paris. I do not have to bustle to a particular spot there; I can savor the city in any quarter, but I had never before visited it in the spring. Since it is inconceivable to me that I shall not visit Paris again, I said to myself as we drove along, "From now on I'll always come in the spring."

Sunday, the third of May, was warm and in full sunlight. The markets were open, the streets were crowded; the customers of the sidewalk cafés were sipping their apéritifs. It was preposterous, of course, to wonder whether it could be the same apéritif that was being sipped when I was last in Paris, in 1949. But knowing something of the length of time a Frenchman can allot to a drink, the idea did cross my mind.

I asked the other two if they knew what part of the city we were in. They said they didn't and were trying to orient themselves. None of us had come in before by way of Orly Field.

At the very instant we were pooling our ideas as to our where-abouts, the driver rounded a corner into the Place de l'Odéon, and there facing the Odéon Theater that is now a branch of the Comédie Française, was the restaurant, the Méditerranée, where the seafood is wonderful and the view at night of the lighted square and theater in the shadow can distract a diner even from his shell-fish.

We passed the Sorbonne where I had taken courses for several summers, and the Cluny Museum across the way, where in 1923 the sight on the same day of a statue, Leda and the Swan, and a Ceinture de Chastité had revealed to me for the first time but with dazzling clarity the biological functioning of the male and female.

I heard Sophy say sharply, "Phew—that's not very pleasant, is it?"

Startled, I looked where she and Zella were pointing to a sign chalked on the wall of a building. It read, "Go home, America."

We looked at one another in dismay and then back again. There was another. "Go back, Ridgway," and next to it, "Get out, Americans."

We were subdued and silent. There seemed to be nothing any one of us could think of to say.

It was good to come out explosively from a narrow street, our driver sounding an hysterical tattoo on his horn, to the quais, the bookstalls and the Seine.

I do absurd things in Paris, the kind of thing I did as a child in the Muncie days when I knew the moment had come for a birthday cake to be brought into the dining room, I always looked away and then back again, very slowly. I liked seeing the cake that way.

On that sunny Sunday morning, the third of May, as we turned onto the quais, I looked at the back of the chauffeur's head, and then very slowly to the left, and saw the proud pointing finger that is the Eiffel Tower. Let anyone else's heart leap up with Words-worth at the sight of a rainbow; I choose the Eiffel Tower, Notre Dame, the Arc de Triomphe, the Place de la Concorde, and Sacré Coeur on the top of Montmartre. I saw them all, except Sacré Coeur.

Zella dropped Sophy and me at the Ritz. She was to stay with friends.

Considering the fact that the Ritz was the only hotel in Paris that could give us a room, it ill behooved me to be churlish about stopping there. But when I go to Europe I have the preposterously sentimental fancy to keep my surroundings as nearly as possible as they were on my first trip. Then I had occupied a room on the fourth floor of a pension. I reached it in the daytime by walking up three flights of stairs, and at night by taking those same flights on the double, because of a hazardous invention of the French called the "*minuterie*." This is a light in the downstairs center hall that, when set to work by pushing a button, maintains an illumination for exactly one minute, at the end of which time it clicks off automatically. If the unlucky pensionnaire is caught halfway to his room at the end of the minute, he must either grope the rest of the way up in pitch blackness, or, feeling his way down to the light button again, renew the whole process, hoping for a better speed record.

The Hotel Félix in Paris had been in the early days my alternate to the pension. Its proprietors, Madeleine and Nicholas, have become dear friends and I have spent gloriously happy days there, and nights running the gantlet from *minuterie* to bedroom. I've counted only as additional fun, the eccentric location of the W.C. on a landing midway between *minuterie* and bedroom. In 1949 I had taken my daughters there.

The pension no longer exists; Madeleine and Nicholas have retired to the country. "*Nous ne sommes pas*," they had written to me, "*éternelles*."

Other hotels of that level had no accommodations for us. The Ritz had increased my distrust of it by cabling extravagantly that a room was being held for us.

A good deal of service accompanied our transfer from the taxi to our quarters. In America, any less service would have displeased me. In Paris, such attention caused my lip to curl. Once established I admitted grudgingly to Sophy that our bedroom was comfortable, but though the W.C. was in its conventional location in the bathroom adjoining our bedroom, I considered the size of the room excessive.

By the time we had washed, unpacked a little and gone down to lunch, it was three o'clock. In a happy flurry at speaking French, I confided to the waiter my decision to eat light for personal reasons having to do with my digestion after a journey on an airplane. I ordered hot soup, cold chicken and a green salad. The waiter asked if I preferred an "*aile*." This seemed to me the last touch of chichi and I told him tartly I really didn't care so long as it was white meat. He seemed surprised, but bowed. Sophy had the kindness to allow him to get out of hearing before she explained, with a good deal of pleasure, that he had asked if

I preferred a wing, not a "she." There ought to be more difference, I protested, between the pronunciation of "*elle*" and "*aile*."

I ruminated during lunch on the lecture I had given the preceding winter on an extensive tour; the theme of this had been the importance of Americans acquiring a speaking knowledge of a foreign language. I wondered if perhaps I was not so bilingual as my fancy had led me to think.

After lunch we walked straight to the Tuileries Gardens and I saw for the first time the horse chestnut trees in full bloom, some pink, and some waxen white. I had always heard them described as looking like tall candelabra with a million tapers, and to my astonishment that is exactly the way they looked. I wasn't prepared for the brilliant color everywhere, flowers and grass. I had always visited Paris in the summer when dust had put over all blooming things a gray topcoat. I knew, too, viewing the crowd, that I had never before seen so many French people there; I had seen other tourists. The French had gone to the country.

They came to the Tuileries Gardens that sunny bright Sunday. It might have been their first outing of the year, the children looked so pale. Their legs were thin, too; their shoes almost without exception, heavy, clumsy, looking as burdensome to walk in on those thin legs as the footgear of a diver. Open booths were everywhere, with balloons, hoops and ices to sell. We walked and walked, not talking much, just looking.

But tired as we were, we went inevitably to the Louvre without a suggestion of our destination from either of us. I must on each first day in Paris pay my respectful wonder to the Winged Victory. And there she was, at the top of a long flight of stairs—how well the French know how to dramatize their treasures. Looking at her, I was irked as always by the recollection of millions of reproductions scattered throughout the world, and almost always in white. Why aren't they made as she is, the color of sand in the sun?

We came back to the hotel so leg-weary we decided on an early

dinner and straight to bed. Where to dine in Paris is not for me an easy decision to make at any time, but when there is only one night allowed, the choice is painfully difficult. The Vefours? that restaurant hidden at the end of the Palais Royale Garden, where the food is Olympian and the decor of red plush, brocade, ivory and gold panels, glittering chandeliers, is exactly as it was in the days when Balzac occupied his favorite table surrounded by a group of his confreres, and where I may sit if I like, and I do. The Méditerranée we had passed that morning on the Place de l'Odéon where seafood is the *spécialité*? Or all the way out to Neuilly, to the Avenue de Neuilly, Number 195? There is the restaurant du Progrès. Dining there guarantees a blissful memory. The Café de la Régence is not so special, but the food is good, moderately priced and sitting there I can look across the Place du Théâtre to the Comédie Française. Then there is the Périgourdine at Number 2 Place St-Michel, triple starred in my address book and that means very, very good food.

We settled for none of these. Our decision was for a little restaurant called Quasimodo. It is on the Île de la Cité. We both leaned toward it, partly from the realization we could drive there along the Seine at dusk and bow to Notre Dame. I wanted to go, too, because my daughter, A (Alis), and her husband now, fiancé then, had discovered this restaurant when we were all there in 1949. My other daughter, B (Margaret), had loved it too. I was already a little homesick for them with a special pang at being in Paris without them. To go to the restaurant would be a little like biting down on a tooth that hurt. So we went.

We sat next to three people, their table alongside ours against the wall. One of these diners was an elderly gentleman with a magnificent head, a flowing tie and tweed jacket. With him was a younger couple, the woman dark, pretty, both of them with a look of intelligence and pleasant sophistication. A wide, tall vase of coral carnations separated us. I shall associate, always now, carnations with May in Paris. All day I had seen them on every flower stall, on tables in the tiniest cafés and bistros. The proprietor of Quasimodo, Nicholas, explained proudly that his had come that very day from the Midi, where they grow. But his bunch was so large and so thick, it irked our neighbor of the flowing tie, and so he began making remarks about it, first to his friends, and then, craning his head around one side and the other, to us, asking if we were "deranged" by flowers of such profusion. He offered us each one, assuring us that would thin out the bunch and so open up his vista. His friends smiled, and so did we, accepting a bloom. Conversation began.

In all the months I spend at home traveling about the country on lecture tours, no one ever speaks to me spontaneously; other people engage in conversation, but I am not included. I am not in such quarantine abroad. Soon we were all talking, and in that warmth, the rust began to melt from my French. Presently we were admitting, Sophy and I, our dismay at the signs, "Go home, America." Our companions were appalled, and then vociferous. We must not interpret those as the feeling of France, they protested. Those had been scrawled by "dirty Communists"; true French people hated those signs, erased them wherever they found such sentiments.

The younger man introduced himself as a member of the government, presented his wife, and our neighbor of the carnations and flowing tie, Monsieur Raphaël Lardeur, the greatest designer of stained glass windows in the world. Monsieur Lardeur rose and bowed. Would we, the politician asked when the artist was seated again, allow him to order a bottle of champagne to pledge the affection France felt for America? We would.

Over the champagne, Monsieur Lardeur asserted proudly that he had been to America, and recently. We had by now been joined by another couple, friends of the original three; they had been dining at a near-by table. They assured us Monsieur Lardeur's trip was still a talked-of wonder, since his previous travels had not extended beyond the left bank in Paris, except to go to his place near Chantilly for the summer.

Monsieur Lardeur said he had loved his trip to America; he had been to Woostair, Massashoosetts, where he had designed windows for their church. He had also learned some English—words he had heard and seen everywhere; "smile" and "queek, queek, queek." Everyone in America went "queek, queek" as if there were something exciting around the corner, and there generally was. But nothing was more astounding to him than to be in a hotel with twenty-five hundred rooms, the New Yorkair. His friends doubted the possibility of this, but we corroborated him. He continued, proud in his role of Marco Polo. What they *would* find difficult to believe was that, in every restaurant in America, the first thing a waiter did was to pour one a glass of water, and put *ice* in it, like a ceremony of welcome. As if water and ice could convey a sense of welcome. They shook their heads over this, deploring such a misapprehension. But everything else, Monsieur Lardeur assured them, was, in America, a miracle.

The meal and the bottle of champagne ended. Sophy and I were urged to let them show us a little of their beloved quarter. And certainly we allowed ourselves to be urged. The new couple who had joined us turned out to be a doctor and his wife, completely charming.

We went to a little café where, we were told, many of the intellectuals gathered. I had a "limonade" and as I sipped it, the doctor's wife asked if we in America knew of Sartre and Existentialism. I assured her we did, and added that I had recently been on a TV program, discussing Mlle. de Beauvoir's book *The Second Sex*. She promptly reported this to the assemblage and it launched a fine discussion. Then we were asked to go to a very special place —one of the very old *caves* of Paris, where there was singing and where much of the talent of the French theater originated.

Of course we went; to the Place Michelle, down a narrow way, through a doorway so small one could scarcely get through it head on; down, down narrow dark stone steps, so old there was a deep hollow in the center of each. We emerged in a vaulted cellar, lighted by candles; people at tables, scarcely discernible in the candlelight. We heard excellent singing, but my French was not up to the words. My friends, learning this, were vastly relieved but said, by way of defense for them, that the songs were very old. I was introduced as an international *radioartiste*, which would have surprised CBS considerably, but I acknowledged the introduction with a brief speech and a firm refusal to sing. Monsieur Lardeur was more obliging. He was, in fact, impatient to be asked. He delivered a song from the stage and in a roaring bass. Returning to the table he leaned toward Sophy and me to say with courteous solicitude he hoped we had not understood the words.

By this time I was awash with lemonade and beginning to feel a bit fatigued. So we said good night. The doctor and his wife drove us home after we had made an appointment to visit Monsieur Lardeur's studio the following morning, and we asked the doctor's wife to lunch with us.

The early night in Paris ended at 2:30 A.M.

Chapter 4

THE FOLLOWING morning at eleven o'clock we left our taxi at the entrance to a deep courtyard on the rue de Cherche-midi. While we were debating whether to penetrate the court or try one of the buildings on either side, we heard a boisterous shout of "Allo, allo," and turning, saw Monsieur Lardeur coming toward us up the street. He took off his hat, waved it round his head and quickened his pace. By the time he reached us he was a little out of breath from this double exertion, but geniality itself.

Awaiting our arrival, he explained, he had gone up the street to a little bistro where he had told the proprietor he would bring two ladies later in the morning for an apéritif. He was leading the way into the court as he spoke, down a passageway with doorways on either side. An old woman coming out of one of these with a basket on her arm said, "Good morning," and he paused to introduce us. A few feet farther on the passage ended and we were at the entrance to the courtyard itself that we had glimpsed from the street. It was broad, open to the sky, and gleaming with sunlight; flagstones covered the greater part of it, but in the center rose a vigorous and fairly large tree. It took me the time of two deep breaths in that piercing sunlight to see that there were about thirty birds perched on the branches, most of them pigeons, but there were warblers and tiny finches.

"Twenty-seven," Monsieur Lardeur said happily when I mentioned this.

Sophy asked if he'd counted them.

"But of course. They are mine," was his answer.

A slender woman came toward us from the passageway. She was not young but her hair was black, parted in the middle, and drawn severely down on either side to a knot in the back. Her skin was olive in color, clear and fine textured. I thought as she came toward us how right she was to wear her hair that way. It revealed the lovely shape of her head and fine bone texture of her face.

"My wife," said Monsieur Lardeur, and she smiled shyly.

We shook hands.

"We were talking about the birds," Sophy said. "Monsieur Lardeur says they all belong to you."

Madame Lardeur forgot her shyness. Her eyes lighted up. "Oh yes," she said, "they live here." She pointed up and behind her. We saw a row of casement windows above the passageway and looking out on the courtyard. In each window was a stack of cages, one on top of the other.

I asked if they came back to their cages at night.

Madame Lardeur shook her head vigorously. "Oh no, I will bring them in very soon," she told us. "I give them two hours exercise in the morning and an hour late in the afternoon. If they were out longer than that they might grow curious to see more of the world and perhaps not come back."

Sophy said it must be very difficult to get them back to their cages. How in the world did she accomplish it?

Madame Lardeur looked surprised. "I call them," she said simply. "They come."

After this announcement I was not unduly surprised to learn the household also included something like nine cats and five dogs, and that in a few weeks the entire household would be taken by a truck hired for the occasion to the Lardeurs' little country place near Chantilly.

Monsieur Lardeur was showing signs of impatience to move us on to his studio, making thrusts with his right arm toward a building at the back of the court, walking a few steps in that direction and then returning. Madame Lardeur said she must go back to the house. She hoped we had found ourselves well amused the preceding evening.

We assured her it had been one of the most delightful experiences we had had in a very long time. We were sorry she had not been there.

She smiled across us indulgently at her husband. "No," she said, "I do not go out in the evenings. I prefer to be at home and my husband prefers to talk with his friends without me. We have four children, you know. That can sometimes engulf a man. Last night," she added, "I was a little disquieted because he is not usually so late. But when he came in he was very gay and woke me to tell me about you and how necessary it had been to show you the friendship of France for America because of those dirty Communists with their shameful writings on the wall."

As she shook hands with each of us, she added earnestly, "Please do not give them the importance of paying attention to the foolish things they say."

Madame Lardeur returned to the house and Monsieur Lardeur hurried us on to the back of the court and through a doorway there.

The sudden change from the glittering courtyard to the dim, cool interior required a little refocusing again, and then I saw we were in a sizable room, perhaps twenty feet long and just as wide. Down the center of this stretched a trestle table of such width as to allow only a passageway around it. The surface of the table was completely covered with what looked to be an enormous jigsaw puzzle made up of pieces in sizes that varied from the dimensions of a piece in an ordinary puzzle to pieces perhaps ten inches long. The wall behind this table and facing us, was solidly filled with

open-faced cupboards, partitioned like large cubbyholes. In each
of these were panes of glass. Monsieur Lardeur moved us on.

"We come back to this later," he said.

We followed him almost the length of the trestle table and in
his wake turned left through a wide arch into a studio at right
angles to the room we had entered. The ceiling of the studio was
certainly thirty feet high. The wall facing us was filled by a stained
glass window, predominantly in dark blues, soft greens, rose and
flecks of yellow. The sun came through this and made a pattern on
the floor that shimmered and shifted like the kaleidoscopes children look through.

Sophy and I had been chattering in the other room, asking
about the jigsaw puzzle and the cubbyholes filled with glass. We
stopped talking, looked at each other and back again at the window. I think she was overwhelmed like me by the actual realization that the gay companion of the night before, who had sung
a naughty song in a *cave*, the resident of the Latin Quarter known
in every bistro, the absurd householder with his birds and dogs
and cats, was a great artist of profoundly religious expression.

I don't know whether it was Sophy or I who spoke first, murmuring gropingly about the penetrating, enveloping light.

Monsieur Lardeur had been silent with us; he answered this
quickly and happily. "But yes," he said, "light and music and
faith; those are the three greatest things in the world. I dream
about, and some day I will make a film of those three things." He
pointed a little to the left of the window. There against the wall
stood a cottage organ, so small a child could have reached all the
keys. Monsieur Lardeur does not weigh under 250 pounds. He
walked over to the tiny instrument and patted it. "It plays," he
said. "Now look behind you," he requested, "that is the beginning."

On the wall he indicated were hung strips of brown wrapping
paper, that pinned together, went from the floor to the skylight.
On these were figures drawn in charcoal. "I show you," the

artist explained, "how I commence." He moved a ladder into position in front of these sketches, mounted it quickly and took
from a hook attached to the top of the ladder, a long pointer. I
had last seen one of these at the Berlitz School. But inserted into
the hollowed-out tip of this one was a piece of charcoal. Holding
the pointer at arm's length, Monsieur the inventor demonstrated
how he drew his preliminary sketches.

Descending the ladder with alarming agility, he took us to the
table in the room we had first entered, bent over its surface and
lifted one of the pieces of glass in the jigsaw puzzle. Underneath
was a piece of brown paper such as we had seen on the walls,
with a portion of a charcoal sketch on it. "You see," he showed
us, "each piece of glass is cut exactly the size of the paper pattern."

I asked how he decided the shape and sizes in which to cut
the paper. He straightened up from the table, looked across at me,
thought for a moment and then shrugged his shoulders. "One
knows," he said.

I admonished myself to be careful what I said lest I betray
my sense of the incongruity of this man facing me; stocky, stout,
wearing a corduroy jacket, a polka dot, bright blue bow tie of
voluminous folds, on his head a felt hat with an astonishingly
wide brim and crown; very large and very black, horn-rimmed spectacles, and the trademark of a Frenchman, a cigarette attached
the Lord knows how to one corner of his mouth; but this man
was not painting robust scenes of life in the Latin Quarter. He
was an artisan and an artist of the Middle Ages, fashioning with
precision and delicacy a form of art that had nothing to do with
Paris or the world.

I turned away from the table and saw for the first time a stained
glass window in that room. This one was framed and hanging
on the wall in a corner by the door from the courtyard. It had the
same qualities as those of the window in the other room, qualities
that had silenced Sophy and me, something mystic, withdrawn,
luminous, with an unearthly light.

Sophy and Monsieur Lardeur joined me in front of it. "That one," he said, "won a prize, but it lives here. I do not let it go." Suddenly he was brisk. "Come," he said, "you can sit down in the other room. I will find my son. You must meet him. Then we go for our apéritif." He trotted out into the courtyard.

In the other room Sophy and I sat down obediently to wait. Our conversation was brief. "Well, I'll be damned," Sophy said.

"Yes," was my answer.

She looked up at the window again. My eye was caught by something yellow on a little table beside me. I saw it was a copy of *L'Illustration* for the seventeenth of January. Since it was the only piece of reading matter in the whole atelier I wondered how it happened to be there. I picked it up and it opened immediately to an article entitled *"Un Curieux Homme"* and underneath it a subtitle "RAPHAEL LARDEUR, MAITRE VERRIER DU XXe SIECLE, PER-PETUE LA TRADITION DES ARTISANS MEDIEVAUX." The illustrations were photographs of the room in which I was sitting; a picture of Monsieur Lardeur on top of the stepladder indicating with pointer a charcoal drawing. I turned the page. There was Monsieur Lardeur in corduroy coat, flowing bow tie, horn-rimmed spectacles, felt hat, cigarette at the corner of his mouth, and he was leaning over the table in the other room picking up one of the pieces of the paper pattern. Underneath this the article ended with a quotation from the artist. *"Il n'y a pas plus beau métier que le mien, pas plus belle matière que la lumière."*

I had no time to read the article nor even show it to Sophy. Monsieur Lardeur was back again, and following him a very handsome, somber-looking young man, with black hair like his mother's. Although the day was warm he was wearing a full-length woolen robe, tied with a cord around his waist. It was a burnoose complete with hood down the back, I saw as he passed me to bow over Sophy's hand. Apart from acknowledging our introduction, he did not speak. Evidently his father had neither expected nor wished anything more, because the instant the introductions were

made, he said we must be on our way for the apéritif. He had perhaps only wanted us to see his oldest son.

On the way back through the courtyard, Monsieur Lardeur
allowed us to pause a moment in the doorway to the big workroom
where, he explained, the glass was cut and put together. After that,
he said, he painted on the completed whole, the finishing details.

The little bistro where we had our apéritif was up the street, perhaps half a block. On the way Monsieur Lardeur was hailed af-
fectionately by every passerby. While Sophy and I sipped Dubonnet
and chatted with the proprietor, Monsieur Lardeur set off to find
his car. He wanted, he had declared, to give himself the pleasure
of driving us back to our hotel, but we must wait a little instant
because he had parked his car somewhere in the vicinity, but at the
moment could not remember exactly what spot. It would therefore take a little reconnoitering, during that time we would amuse
ourselves with a Dubonnet. We had not quite finished when he
drew up at the curb blowing his horn.

The drive was agonizing. Monsieur Lardeur put his hands to the
wheel only at such rare moments when he was not either pointing
out a sight for us or hailing a friend. His method of crossing intersecting streets was one with which I was not familiar, but that
evidently pleased him because he explained it.

"I do not like to stop at a corner," he said, "because then I do
not see adequately what is coming from either side. Therefore, as
you notice, I move into the middle of the crossing street. There I
stop and look carefully, to left and to right."

"I like also," he confided a little farther on, "to have some gaiety
with the young girls that pass in front of my car. I greet them, tell
them they are pretty and they will surely one day have a fine
husband. Old women I do not care for, therefore I like to scare
them with my horn." I had noticed this.

The moment we crossed the bridge over the Seine to the right
bank, his whole manner changed. He became cautious, even timid.
I counted this a change vastly for the better. "Here I am a

stranger," he told us. "You must show me the way. Now what is this hotel where you stop?"

"The Ritz," Sophy told him.

"I do not know it," he said. "You will show me how we must go to reach there."

We directed him through each crossing and around each turn. He drove slowly looking neither to the left nor the right. But when we emerged into the Place Vendôme, he lifted both hands above his head. "Let us see," he said, "this is splendid. This has beauty, this place."

I ventured to ask if he had never seen it before. "But of course I have not," he said. "I live on the left bank. Now, however, I shall come again. I must bring my wife and my children. This is beautiful, this has space and light."

He started the car again but did not go out of first speed because, he explained, he wished to see everything. Accordingly, we completed the circle of the Place on the lurch. We made one other stop before we reached the Ritz. "There," Monsieur Lardeur said pointing to a window, "is an establishment very well known. I have heard of it. You must note it. It is considered very fine."

We noted it, Sophy and I. It was Cartier's show window.

As we stood on the curb in front of the Ritz saying our good-bys and our thanks, Monsieur Lardeur leaned well out of the car to view the façade of the hotel. He nodded his head several times. "This must be an excellent hotel," he pronounced, "to be in such a beautiful place. You are without doubt wise to come here."

He took my hand and Sophy's in each of his. "*Au revoir*," he said, "and when you return you will come to see me and then I will come back here to see this again."

At the doorway, we turned back for a last look. Monsieur Lardeur, leaning far out one side of his little car, was circling the Place again.

Chapter 5

THE SIMPLON ORIENT EXPRESS for Venice leaves the Gare de Lyons in Paris at seventeen-fifty in the evening, but on Monday the fourth of May, Sophy and I very nearly missed it. We were ready in good time but we waited on the sidewalk in front of the rue Cambon entrance of the Ritz. Our bags were piled around us while the doorman, porters and two other employees we had never seen before but who had joined our departure for a tip, ran to either end of the street and hallooed to one another their inability to see a taxi. After a length of time that brought Sophy and me to a condition of resigned despair, the heralds returned to us for a conference and for the reiteration of the absence of any *voitures.*

During this tohubohu a taxi drew up. The driver leaned out and shouted into the tumult asking if his services were required. As we rocketed across Paris and in the short spaces between the hysterical tattoos our driver was sounding on his horn, I asked him why taxis were so scarce. I did this partly out of curiosity and greatly as a distraction from the contemplation of imminent death. It was not a good idea for distraction. The chauffeur, answering, turned around to look at me, causing Sophy fervently to voice the wish that either I would keep my trap shut or let her out. However, I did learn that there are not enough taxi drivers in Paris to

46

provide two shifts, and that the working day is eleven hours long. At the end of that time the driver must turn in his cab unless he secures a new passenger before 6 P.M. In that event he can stay out until the passenger no longer requires his services, even if that is past midnight.

Zella was waiting for us at the gate to the train, wild of eye and short of breath, giddy from indecision. For twenty minutes, she said, gasping, she had been on the lope to and from the entrance of the station watching for our arrival and trying to make up her mind to go on without us.

We were on the run down the platform as Zella recited her anxiety and activity, but neither lack of wind nor heat of temper can stay Zella from her accustomed volubility. Our porters caught up with us. There were three of them and they were all shouting—encouragement, we thought, but it turned out to be the news that we had not picked up the proper slip of paper that entitled us to pass through the gates and board the train.

Zella took off on the instant, still talking. Thank God she is a beautiful athlete. I doubt, however, that on the running track in the Bryn Mawr gymnasium she ever set a better record than from train to station and back again. And we made the train.

Sophy's and my compartments were adjoining; Zella's farther down the carriage. Once our bags were properly distributed we joined up and went at once to the dining car. We congratulated one another, on the way, on our congeniality, evidenced by our unanimous assertion that food would bring us the quickest recovery from what we had just been through.

At the doorway to the restaurant car the steward asked for our tickets. Each of us delved into and groped about in her knapsack that is the form of pocketbook the American woman carries abroad, and each produced her railroad ticket. The steward was not interested in these. What he required, he explained, was our ticket for reservations in the dining car. We hadn't any, we told him. That, he answered, was impossible. How does that pass itself, he inquired. Because, I told him piteously, no one had told us such a thing was necessary. We were Americans, and therefore ignorant, and no one had been of assistance to us in such a matter.

He admitted us at once, overcome at our unhappy situation and the lack of feeling on the part of those in France who, unlike himself, had kept us in ignorance of these important regulations. He swept us past disgruntled passengers waving their tickets at him, and gave us an excellent table.

Dinner was more than excellent, it was beautiful. Had there been a menu I would have brought it home, ordered it mimeographed and sent a copy to every railroad in the United States. We were served *une bonne potage*, then a delicate fish, rolled and with a shrimp sauce; after that tenderloin of beef, string beans, a crisp green salad, ice cream, that we declined, cheese and fruit, and a bottle of wine. The price for all this as I remember, including the wine, was about two dollars apiece. Zella, who has a tendency to be practical, endeavored to compute, from the number of courses, how many dishes had to be washed.

We went to bed immediately after dinner. We were numb with drowsiness. The last thing I said standing in the door of my compartment was, "Do you realize we're actually on the Orient Express? Shades of Agatha Christie and E. Phillips Oppenheim!"

Some hours later I was wakened by a light on my face. I sat up, too scared to yell though I opened my mouth. I looked into the face of a man who stepped back a pace hastily, at my sudden uprising, and bowed. He then showed me a cardboard case of some sort he was holding in his left hand, dropped it on the bed beside me, bowed again, wheeled around, switched off his flashlight, opened the door and was gone. I lay down, rigid with fright, too terrified to turn on the light or call for help. I groped around on the bed, found the little case and shoved it under my pillow. And because the lack of rest for three nights preceding this one brought complete exhaustion, I fell asleep again in the very middle of my terror.

I was awakened by a pounding on the wall, and Sophy's voice through the partition, urging me to raise the blind and look out. I did. It was early morning and I saw Stresa on Lake Maggiore, snow-covered mountains in the distance, white bullocks in a field, a donkey cart driven along a road by a man wearing on his head a gay, bright red bandana, overhead a pale blue sky, tinged with pink and sunrise. And being an old fool I wept a little.

I was blowing my nose when I remembered what had happened the night before. I pounded on the partition, put my face against it and asked Sophy in as loud a whisper as I dared use, if she could come in at once. I needed her, I said.

She was tying a belt around her dressing gown when I opened the door to her. She peered at me and demanded to know at once if I was sick. I told her impatiently I was perfectly well, pulled her inside, and shut the door. We sat down on the bed.

"Listen," I said, "I don't expect you to believe this. It's pure Agatha Christie. I wish to God I'd never mentioned her name last night, but I swear to you a man got into my compartment in the middle of the night and he handed me a package of papers. He had a flashlight and he woke me up by turning it on my face. I don't know what on earth is going on and I certainly don't intend to get you involved in it, but I'm going to the American Consul the very first thing. I'm not getting myself mixed up with any international spies. And why on earth would they pick on me, anyway?"

Sophy was staring at me. "You *are* sick," she said. "You're out of your mind."

I smiled at her. "I don't blame you," I told her. "But just let me show you something." I reached under my pillow, and pulled out my own passport.

Between spasms of silly hilarity she reminded me that before going to bed last night we had handed our passports to the porter who had requested them for the customs man; he would check them sometime during the night. I had been too dazed with fatigue at the time, I realized, either to take in what the porter said, or to remember it later. Acknowledging this to Sophy I demanded to know, however, how the customs man, if that's what he really was, had got in my compartment. I did remember locking my door, I insisted.

"The porter has a passkey," was Sophy's answer. "He told you that, too. Italians aren't bothered by any nonsense about privacy. They're very thoughtful people. They don't inconvenience you by making you get up and open the door. They come in."

Our dining car of the night before had been removed somewhere along the line. A new one for breakfast was added at Milan. For this reason our stop there was longer than at other stations. I walked on the platform a few minutes and then came back to stand in the corridor and lean out the windows; one of the pleasantest occupations, I think, and possible only on European trains. I wish American ones were designed that way.

It was a little tantalizing to look out on as much of Milan as I could see beyond the station from the train window, knowing that in a few days I would be getting off a train in that same station, moving up the stairs I was looking at, and on beyond, to spend a day and night in that city on the way to Rome. But that would happen on Friday, and we would have been three days in Venice.

Some of the people I had seen going up the stairs came back and boarded the train in the third-class carriages. Each one was carrying sandwiches made with thick crusty rolls, a large piece of cheese unwrapped, and a bottle of Chianti. This was evidently the standard breakfast on sale in the station.

Sophy joined me at the window and I pointed out to her these provisions. I said it looked to me like a wonderful meal except for the Chianti. Sophy's answer was that it looked wonderful to her without any qualifications, and regretted she had not known about it in time to get those supplies from the station for the three of us. But as we were talking, the guards were shouting, doors were banging, the train began to move.

A genteel knocking on the door to Zella's compartment brought no response. Sophy standing behind me suggested I try the door, reminding me what she had said about lack of privacy. The door opened easily. We both went in and found Zella sound asleep. We sat on her bed while she dressed and Sophy saw fit to tell her my encounter in the night and my mistaken interpretation of it, adding that she herself had been roused by a tap on the door, had answered and been given time to put on her dressing gown and admit the customs man. They had had a short but pleasant conversation while he inspected her passport.

"In Italian?" I asked.

"Certainly," she told me smugly.

"What did you tell him?" I asked, "that the hat was on the chair and the pen was on the table?"

"We talked about Italy," Sophy said. "It was very interesting."

Zella had stopped dressing and was looking from one to the other of us in obvious bewilderment. She rushed into speech before Sophy had finished. "What on earth are you talking about?" she demanded. "People coming into your compartments. Nobody came into mine. My passport hasn't been stamped, that's all. They probably won't let me off at Venice. Why didn't one of you come and get me?"

While I was protesting that in the state of fright I had been in I doubted I could have got out of bed at the cry of "Fire," Zella was ringing violently for the porter.

He answered the peremptory call almost at once. Zella broke into his "Good morning" with a vehement recital of her predicament delivered with the speed of a machine gun in action. She was on the second round before the porter understood what she was saying, and he held up his hands in protest, smiled, and she stopped.

"But the customs man did come last night, Signora," he said in careful English. "I gave him your passport. He entered your cabin. I come, too. He put on his light, we both look at you. You are sleeping so quietly, so happily, like a little child, your face is turned away, but we agree it is a pity to rouse you. The customs officer takes my word it is your photograph on the passport, and we go. I notice your cover is disarranged," he added, "so I return and replace it. It was chilly." He drew a passport from his pocket and handed it to Zella. "Is stamped."

"*Grazie*," Sophy said.

Zella took the passport.

We had a table companion at breakfast. He was gray-haired and dressed in a cheap but clean suit, a shirt without a tie but buttoned at the neck. His hands were thick, the nails broken, the skin cracked, the fingers on one twisted and crippled. He joined our conversation announcing himself an American. He was friendly, and not too friendly. He asked where we came from and where we were going. And we in turn asked the same things of him. He was on his way to Yugoslavia, he told us, and spoke very broken English. He was returning to the little town his family had come from. I asked how long it had been since he had visited it, and he told us he had never been there. I asked if he came from another part of Yugoslavia, and he answered with some surprise and a little annoyance that of course not, he was an American, born in Montana. He had been to Europe only once and that was as a soldier in the First World War. For the last ten years he had lived in Cleveland, working in a factory there. Now he was on his way to see the brothers and sisters that had been left behind when the family had emigrated before his birth. And he added, beaming, "I take American clothes for all of them. I never see them; I do not know sizes, but they will like."

I began to picture what his life in America must have been; always I supposed in a colony of the countrymen of his parents. This was the only way I could account for his difficulty with English. I wondered why public school education had not enforced a knowledge of our language and concluded he must have had very little of it.

He finished breakfast and said good-by, shaking hands with each of us. "Many, many Americans like me on train," he said as he left, "all going home to Yugoslavia for first time."

And then I knew what the unfamiliar accent was I had heard around me on the platform in the station at Milan, the language of Americans like him, going home to Yugoslavia for the first visit.

The three of us finished our breakfast without conversation. We were looking out the windows at vineyards as far as the eye could reach; each vine strung between what looked like two stunted trees about four feet high. Once we passed a farm, a pair of white bullocks drawing a wagon in a field beside it, and in front of the farmhouse a high, sunny yellow wall with a peach tree espaliered against it. Always the Dolomites in the distance. And once Sophy pointed out irrigation ditches across a field, but I was the first to see a double row of cypress trees.

Forty plus years make a considerable stretch of waiting for a first glimpse of cypress trees in Italy. People in Indiana use a wistful phrase. It is "get to go." I never thought I'd get to go to Italy, and see cypress trees in a row, but I'm here, I said to myself. And out loud, "Well, forevermore."

Chapter 6

STANDING IN front of the railway station at Venice, at a little after noon on Tuesday, May 5, I suddenly remembered an O. Henry story I had read years ago. It was the story of a widely traveled and very rich young man. He fell in love with a young woman who had scarcely any money at all and had not traveled beyond the Island of Manhattan. In his proposal of marriage the hero sought to dazzle her by the prospect of a honeymoon in Venice, and he described it. But the heroine turned him down because, as she told her chums later, she was not going to tie herself up to any cheap skate who offered as a honeymoon to take her through the tunnel of love at Coney Island.

I hadn't thought of that story in a long time; neither had I been in Venice for twenty-five years. At this reunion I knew that girl was my kin. It wasn't true that I was walking out of a railway station and down a flight of steps to a dock where a black gondola taxi was waiting. I laughed aloud, and Sophy and Zella who were a little ahead of me turned back and laughed too. I didn't have to repeat the O. Henry story to them. The first sight of Venice, I think, brings, from everyone, a spontaneous sound of incredulous delight.

The porters piled our luggage into the high prow, the gondolier and porters helped each of us into the boat, the gondolier took up

his stand in the stern, and the taxi was under way. Our taxi driver wore on his head a wide-brimmed hat of soft straw. Indicating it, I confided to my companions that I had worn one just like it as a child for a "best." His had a wide ribbon band around it, bright red, with streamers down the back. So did mine, I said, except that my ribbon was black velvet; his was much smarter.

The launches that passed us fussily and pulled in to docks where passengers were taken on, others unloaded, were Venice trolley cars, of course. I pointed them out to Zella, and she laughed again. We didn't laugh when we saw ahead of us a bridge higher than others we had gone under, and rimmed with little shops. "The Rialto?" I asked our gondolier. It was, of course.

The main section of the Royal Danieli Hotel was once the Palazzo of the Doge Enrico Dandolo. I think the Doge must have given word to his artisans that the best was none too good for him and that the more of it they could include in the decoration, the better pleased he would be. The result is a giddy splendor.

Zella, Sophy and I had a suite, a double room and a single, each opening on our own hallway, and at the end of this a bath. The window of the bath gave on a large stair well that ran from the lobby below us to the top of the building. Conversation floated up to us. We learned very quickly not to make this reciprocal.

Within half an hour of our arrival we were at lunch in the Terrace Restaurant on the roof and I ate Scampi for the first time, that European delicacy something like our crayfish. My memorandum of that day reads: "Order Scampi whenever it is on a menu." Bread, cheese and a glass of wine made up the rest of our meal.

It was while we were waiting for lunch to arrive that Zella established herself as a traveling companion with unusual equipment. Plunging into her bag for her cigarette case, she produced in sequence and laid on the table, a pair of binoculars, a flashlight and a compass. They had been given her, she explained, as going away presents and she was sure we would find them very useful.

"For instance," she said bending over the compass, "I haven't set
foot on the streets of Venice as yet, but when I do I'll at least
know in what direction I'm heading. At the moment, in case
you're interested, I'm facing due southeast."

Sophy answered she was not only interested, she was fascinated,
because Zella had certainly put the sun in an extraordinary place
for that hour of the afternoon. Zella returned the compass to her
pocketbook, but guaranteed she would get the hang of it with a
little practice and we would all be grateful to her. It would make
a pretty sight, I told her, the rest of us wandering through cathe-
drals and art galleries, guidebook in hand, Zella with her compass
motionless on a fixed spot getting her bearings so we would know
where we were. "And no doubt," Zella added, "the rest of you
using my binoculars, maybe my flashlight, on your wanderings,
while I'm working for you."

Sophy interrupted this happy speculation. "I'd like to talk about
money," she said abruptly, "if you don't think that's too sordid.
But I have an idea about it."

I assured her I was delighted to hear any idea about money at
any time. Zella declared with some bitterness that she'd always
considered herself very capable about money, but her husband
had sent her off with so many kinds of it; cash, American Express
checks, letter of credit, another kind of letter to a banker friend in
London in case of emergency, francs in one compartment of her
purse, lire in another, American dollars in a position to make her
stomach bulge; by now she felt awash with money with no ideas
about any of it. It wasn't, she added apologetically, that she had so
much, it was just that it was so distributed.

Sophy explained her idea. In her opinion, she said, there was
no more dismal sight than a group of women at a table in a
restaurant recapitulating the entire meal in order to estimate what
each one owed—who had taken dessert, how many had had coffee,
all this time a waiter standing by, and at the end a final flurry
about making change, how much to tip, with incoherent leaps

into a calculus of: If Mary would pay the tip that would make up for the stamp she had borrowed from Sally and they would deduct the remainder from what Sally would owe at the next meal. "It's not only a shame-making sight to everybody else in the restaurant," Sophy added, "that kind of haggling can blast lifelong friend-ships."

There was no argument about this. If she had any solution I begged her to get on with it.

"Well," she began, "this is my idea. Why don't we all put an equal amount of money into a general pot? Let one of us be the banker, so to speak; pay for meals, tips, hotel rooms, everything except what each of us individually buys. When the pot is empty, we all put up more money. Of course it won't be exactly even," she admitted, "but anyone who makes a habit of ordering specials can put up the difference, and we'd concede lesser discrepancies, such as somebody ordering orange juice for breakfast and some-body else not; let all those go by."

Zella and I were providing a chorus of little cries of pleasure and encouragement, until Zella became articulate enough to interrupt Sophy. "Won't it be an awful job for the banker?"

Sophy said she didn't think so and promptly offered to take on the job herself if we would like to have her. "I know you could do it easily," she said to Zella, "but I hate to dump it on you since it was my idea. As far as Emily is concerned," she added, "that's out."

She turned to me. "You couldn't even *count* the money we'd give you," she explained kindly. "It's no reflection on your efforts, it's just that your mathematics are unreliable."

I told her I was vastly relieved not to have to do even my own spending.

The whole thing was settled then and there, and from that moment until the end of the trip, this was the plan we followed and counted it enormously successful. Sophy kept the mutual funds apart from her own, in a separate container so that she had no intricate figuring to do, and insisted all the way through that she liked her job.

After lunch we went out immediately to see St. Mark's Square. It had taken me twenty-five years to reach it again, but it was just around the corner from the Danieli. Standing at the corner and looking straight ahead, I said, "That's the clock tower," as though the other two didn't know as well as I that it was; as though they hadn't, like me, from early childhood seen pictures of the two giant figures, "The Moors," that stand at the top on either side of a great bell and pound out the hours with bronze hammers.

"I'd forgotten," I said to the others, "how enclosed the square is; it's almost like a tremendous courtyard." I hadn't forgot there would be little café tables and chairs fringing the courtyard, but I hadn't remembered so many. There must have been hundreds.

We walked round and round the square. Occasionally we were tempted to explore an archway leading to a street beyond. But there was so much activity in the square itself, so many shop windows to examine, such an urgent inner need to look closely at the Basilica, and then back away to see it in relation to its neighbors, that we retreated from each impulsive sally beyond the great courtyard deciding it was, at the moment, erratic and irrelevant.

We finally left the square only because of an urge to visit Harry's Bar. Each of us had heard this was *the place* to be at cocktail time. Perhaps we were too early, but we found it dull and self-consciously plain in physical appearance. We drank our apéritifs briskly with no inclination to linger and returned to the hotel, where we napped, bathed and dressed for dinner.

We dined at Qadri's in the piazza. Our table was at a window on the second floor. My meal began with minestrone, and I knew with the first spoonful that every dinner I would eat in Italy would begin with minestrone. After that veal with mushrooms, spinach, bread and cheese for dessert. This set the pattern for the boundaries of dinner for me from that time on. Minestrone to start, bread and cheese to finish, and a bottle of wine. Furthermore that meal dissipated the misgiving I'd had about travel in Italy. I am made violently ill by garlic or onion. I had thought all food in Italy would have this seasoning and had considered taking along canned soups and crackers as my only means of survival. I'd given up this plan because of the weight problem when traveling by air. It was the hand of Providence that stayed me from this excess. At lunch that day, and now at dinner there had been no whiff of garlic nor onion, except a little perhaps in the minestrone, not enough to trouble me. I knew then it could be like this wherever we went; I was safe. I have corroborated this now. No one has to eat garlic or onion in Italy.

Below us on its stand, a band was playing in the square. In close, confusing neighborliness, an orchestra was giving a concert. The chairs at the little tables were filled, the occupants applauded impartially each number rendered by the orchestra, and in turn, the selection from the band. The audience evidently enjoyed the medley provided.

Without any warning that we had heard, a thunderstorm cleared the square. In startling flashes of lightning we could see the musicians bolting from their stands trying to cover with their coats their instruments, and the members of the audience on the run colliding with one another and with waiters who sprang out from the little cafés to drag under cover the chairs and tables.

By the time we had finished eating, the storm was over, but we walked home across a deserted piazza. The moon was out, the wet stones under our feet glistened in the light. We straggled apart, not talking, until Sophy suddenly called to us in a hoarse whisper, "Close in, girls, I'm being followed."

It was not because of an underestimating of Sophy's power of attraction that I was startled. It was only the incongruity of such a threat when three sedate middle-aged women were trudging home together. But Sophy was right. As we flanked her I realized a young admirer was close on her heels and I could hear him murmuring something to her in urgent repetition.

When we came out of the square and turned left toward our hotel I could see him more clearly because the lights were brighter there. My first impression of his youth was right, though I took only a quick sideways glance to reassure myself he was not a menacing cutthroat type. He was not in the least disconcerted by Zella's and my proximity, nor by the number of people crowding the sidewalks on a promenade. Zella and I each inquired solicitously if Sophy had in mind any particular way in which we might help. I volunteered to say, "Shoo," very loud. Zella offered to claim Sophy as her daughter and insist she was a well-brought-up girl just out of the convent, if Sophy would teach her how to say it in Italian. Sophy requested each of us to shut up.

My answer was that in the face of such ingratitude, I would leave her. Zella said she was coming with me, out of tact. She had never been a girl, she declared, to muscle in on anyone's affair, and she certainly was not going to start now.

Sophy's response to both of us was even more impolite than her first one. We left her standing in the middle of the promenade, the young man hovering at her ear, but we paused in the doorway to allow some people to emerge from the revolving door. I'm glad of that pause. It allowed us to see Sophy suddenly do a full about face, confront her pursuer, and to hear her say, "What is the word for grandmother?"

We saw the young man step back startled, put his hand dramatically at his breast, and heard him answer, "I am not grandmother."

And Sophy, smiling, leaned toward him once more. "No," she said sweetly, "but I am," and she patted his head.

Zella and I shot through the revolving door.

When Sophy joined us in the lounge we had ordered three green mint frappés. Her mood had changed. She was cordiality itself as she sat down with us; a little arch, perhaps, I thought, and a touch patronizing. She wanted evidently to convey a romantic parting. She didn't know we'd seen her. She approved our choice of liqueur, endorsing it even to the extent of saying she would probably have two. I saw our waiter come into the room carrying the three crème de menthes on a tray, and looking about uncertainly. The room was crowded, I knew the waiter would have difficulty locating us, so I stood up intending to move toward him.

Simultaneously a man at the table behind us rose to his feet and back to back, we bumped smartly. Instantly we reversed and stood face to face, and each of us said exactly the same thing. "So sorry. Why for heaven's sake. What are you doing here?"

I do not know the reason for this spontaneous but curious greeting on the part of two Americans meeting abroad, but it is invariably given. I gave the conventional answer, too, and so did my partner in the duet.

"We got in just this morning," I said.

And my partner, "We arrived last night."

This is always accepted as a satisfactory explanation of "What are you doing here?"

Each of us turned to our respective tables indicating the other occupants, and there was a flurry of all-around introductions; my friends to Mrs. Nutting, seated at the table, Mr. Harold Nutting, with whom I had collided, and Mr. Walter Luscher, beside Mrs. Nutting.

Our pleasant skirmish had attracted the notice of the waiter with our drinks. He brought them over to us, helped bring the two tables together, and took the orders for their drinks. Like me, Harold Nutting had stood up to signal him. We continued in the pattern all Americans follow when they meet abroad. Questions and answers about places visited, hotel accommodations, exchanges of addresses for good shopping, comparison of prices encountered, disappointment expressed at not having visited places the others had been, and an inner satisfaction with our own selection. I inserted into the conversation a conjecture that the two men had included some business, and explained to Sophy and Zella that

Mr. Nutting is a Vice-President of Marshall Field and Company in Chicago, and Mr. Luscher the head of its European offices. With a tinge of sharpened interest I asked if they were visiting any particular place in Venice.

Mr. Nutting answered. They were going the next morning, he said, to a glass factory from which Marshall Field and Company bought almost the entire output. They had chartered a boat to take them over to the Island of Murano. Would we like to come along?

Mrs. Nutting interrupted, urging us to accept. It would be such a pleasant change for her to have women along so that she could say, "Isn't that lovely?" and to hear what they thought, instead of having to keep still and listen to talk about costs and mark-ups. It was dear of her to be so cordial, but I would have shamelessly asked myself along had I not been invited.

Back in our rooms later, as we were getting ready for bed, I tried to explain this to Sophy and Zella. They knew that Marshall Field's store is my Alma Mater, my very first job had been in that store. But they couldn't know the special smell of smoke to a fire horse that comes to anyone who has worked in a department store. I tried to explain it. "In a department store," I said, "there's an excitement about merchandise that is reborn like the phoenix every time a new shipment comes in. You'd think the buyers would get blasé about it and look at it as just more of the same old stuff coming in season after season. But they don't."

I never before thought why this should be. But I tried to put it into words for Sophy and Zella. "I think maybe," I said, "a buyer is a little like the producer of a play. A buyer has no way of telling whether or not the merchandise he is going to present will sell. If the salespeople don't like the selection, they won't put it over. And the executives, those boys in the front office, are like the backers of a play. They want to get their money back on their investment in the buyer and their production, and every buying trip is a new production. So when the new stuff comes in, it's a whole new uncertainty and excitement.

"I can remember in the midst of getting the Field magazine on the press when a buyer would telephone me in the advertising department with the news that her hats from Paris were being unpacked in the shipping room. Would I like to see them? And I'd drop everything, even in that crisis of going to press, and make for the shipping room on the run.

"I have no such feeling when I go into a store and am on the other side of the counter. But let me hear something like that tonight about going to a factory from which glass is going to come to that shipping room at Field's and I become so excited I feel as if my nose were twitching."

We were in bed, but I continued talking, inspired by a sudden recollection that Mr. Nutting was a stereo camera enthusiast, and that his had been the first pictures from that invention I had seen. This, in turn, had prompted me to give one of these cameras as a wedding present to my son-in-law, Dick. Somewhat shamefacedly I had borrowed it, to bring on this trip, reasoning to both of us in apology that after all it wasn't a first edition of anything and could be replaced, if damaged. Dick had been enthusiastically generous about lending it to me, but disconcertingly less than that about my grasp of how to operate the camera. In spite of a number of lessons from him and, at Dick's urgent request, from a gentleman at the Eastman Kodak store in New York, I had not dared try a picture. I would take my camera along the next day. With Mr. Nutting to show me I would take my first pictures. Wasn't it wonderful he had turned up at the very start of the trip? He could set me properly on my way and I would show Dick when I got home how mistaken his gloomy prophecy of film waste had been. I asked my friends to imagine what a satisfaction it would be when I showed Dick film after film of superb pictures.

There was no response from the next room or the adjoining bed, and I realized I had been talking for some time to myself.

Chapter 7

EARLY NEXT morning I telephoned Mr. Nutting. He is truly an enthusiast; his response to my request that he show me the ways of my camera was a suggestion not to wait until we got to Murano, but to meet him in the lobby as soon as I was dressed and go out for a few preliminary shots in the square.

Zella came into the room while I was making these plans. When I had hung up, she evidenced, by her surprise and pleasure at what she had overheard, that she had, as I'd surmised, been fast asleep the night before during my dissertation. She would like to join us, she said, and bring her own camera. It was not a stereo but there were a number of gadgets that had proved puzzling to her. It belonged to her husband and though he'd consented to her bringing it on the trip, he had evinced some melancholy at the number of films she had purchased, deeming them a fruitless expenditure. She would just like to show him.

We met Mr. Nutting in the hotel lobby and went with him immediately to the spot that must tie with Niagara Falls for the record of the numbers of camera shutters that have been clicked there. This is the site from which can be snapped a narrow canal and over it the Bridge of Sighs. We took up the conventional stance there, each position regulated by the type of camera; Mr. Nutting and I heads up, holding the camera as he directed, pressed against the forehead to insure steadiness, Zella bowed over hers in the more old-fashioned manner. The sun slanted across the water and touched the bridge. Mr. Nutting showed me carefully what exposure to give this lighting, then telling me I had only to push the button, turned to Zella. He didn't know a great deal about her particular make, he told her, but as far as he could see she had everything all right except for one detail. She was holding the camera backward. If she carried out her present focusing, she would achieve an enlarged and highly detailed section of her *"poitrine."* Zella executed a hasty reverse.

From this camera study we moved on to the square. Mr. Nutting, using my camera, photographed Zella and me feeding the pigeons. I am not a traveler who shies away from what is contemptuously termed "touristry." I am a tourist and I follow tourist traditions. I ride in an open carriage in any city that makes a specialty of that type of transportation; I buy postcards, and in St. Mark's Square I fed the pigeons, purchasing a little paper cornucopia filled with corn from one of the vendors that offered them as we approached. I enjoyed attracting, with the corn, the pigeons to settle on my shoulder, head, hand, but in that process I became aware of a phenomenon that I do not understand.

I remember that in Shreveport, Louisiana, there is a certain block on a main street where pedestrians walk only on one side, because the other has been taken over by the pigeons. In Philadelphia, the south side of Locust Street between Broad and Fifteenth is strictly for the birds; people pass along it at considerable risk. But in St. Mark's Square in Venice, the pigeons show a consideration that seems to me unnatural. There is no reminder of them anywhere.

On the way back to the hotel I mentioned to my companions my admiration for these birds, but Zella and Mr. Nutting were engrossed in details of photography and evinced little interest in a natural history phenomenon.

Walter Luscher had gathered up Sophy and Mrs. Nutting.

They were all waiting for us, seated on the deck of an elegant launch that was tied up at the dock by the hotel. We three photographers snapped them, and took more pictures on the short trip to Murano though the day was overcast.

The first thing we noticed as we stepped off the launch was a startling array of Communist posters that covered the façade of every building along the canal. At the sight of these Sophy produced somewhat shamefacedly a camera of her own. It was one of the very cheapest models, she explained to Mr. Nutting, and therefore was not taxing to operate. She added she had not been particularly interested in the Bridge of Sighs as a photographic subject and for that reason had not joined us, but these posters would make an interesting record to show skeptics at home who would not admit it, the prevalence of Communism in Italy. She took an over-all panorama and moved in for a closeup, showing a larger-than-life size head of Malenkov. I found myself looking about furtively in a vague apprehension that an actual Communist might appear from behind the posters and confiscate her camera and us. Nothing of the sort happened; no passerby took the slightest interest in what Sophy was doing. When she had completed her photographic study, we moved on a few yards to a gateway Walter Luscher indicated as the entrance to the glass factory.

Barovier and Toso's is not like any plant I have seen in America. We walked through a beautiful iron gateway and saw to one side the building we were to enter. It looked like an old palazzo of gray stone. Beyond, at the end of a long walk that flanked it, I had a glimpse of a lovely garden.

As we came into the foyer, we saw a broad stairway curving up and out of sight, and two gentlemen descending it. Mr. Luscher met them at the foot of the stairs and introduced them to us. They were the owner of the factory and his son. They both evidenced great pleasure at our visit, counting it an honor to have as a guest the Vice-President of Marshall Field and Company. The son was the more articulate spokesman in English, and requested us to return upstairs with them to look at the studio where the objects were displayed, and from there we would go to the factory proper.

Halfway up the stairs my eye was caught by a large decoration of some sort hanging on the wall, and I paused to look at it. I saw that it was a genealogical chart and that it covered a considerable space. The son stopped beside me and pointing to it said, "That is our family tree. We are glassblowers, father to son, since the thirteenth century."

The objects in the studio itself would have made any woman giddy with avarice. Rows of glittering delicate chandeliers swayed from the ceiling; shelves around the room held candlesticks, vases, bowls, figures; white, colored, large and small.

Fifteen minutes after crossing the threshold I had purchased a chandelier, two pairs of candlesticks and a bowl, thanks to the benevolence of Mr. Nutting who allowed me to be counted still a member of the Marshall Field and Company organization. Zella, Sophy and Mrs. Nutting had taken a lively part in my selections. Mr. Nutting resigned himself to it, observing mildly that it came as no particular surprise. He would like to move us on, however, without further setbacks to the factory proper.

We went downstairs and outside, following a path to the building behind the one we had visited. There were trees and flowers along this path, and as we turned in to the second building, I could see more of the bright garden in the rear than I had glimpsed from the entrance gate.

The interior of the factory was dim except for a dusty golden light that came from open furnaces in a circle around a chimney in the center of the room. Though the day itself was not sunny, we had to wait on the threshold a little to adjust our vision to the relative darkness immediately around us. Then we saw the room proper was large, the floor we were walking on was rough stone; here and there around these furnaces and just out of reach of their heat, were workbenches, each one at some distance from its neighbor. Tools of iron hung in racks on the walls.

The Signors Toso led us to a vantage point at the end of the room by the door, from which we would see the length of the room, and yet, we immediately recognized, be out of danger. The danger threatened us from iron pokers about six feet in length. On the end of each of these hung trembling a large lump, like a bee-hive of molten glass. These were carried by workmen passing to and from the furnaces. The workmen traveled at a pace just under a run. They looked something like knights jousting on foot, except that they did not touch one another. Had they been less dexterous jousters, I thought as I watched them, we would be looking at a body of men mutually impaled on burning glass.

Concentrating finally on one, I followed his passage from the furnace to one of the benches where another workman sat. I saw this one indicate to the courier just where his dangling mass was to be pressed, and saw it fused to an object between a large pair of tongs held in both hands by a third workman. As he indicated this fusion the man rose from the bench and with a tool in each hand began at lightning speed to chip off with one, and smooth with the other. And the man who had brought the globe of glass spun between his hands the poker from which it hung suspended. Then, at a nod from the worker with tools, he withdrew the poker, turned and ran with it back toward the furnace. Instantly, another man took his place with a fresh globe of light. The man with the tools indicated another spot, the globe was gently pressed there; the poker spun in the hands of the man who held it.

I had forgot about anyone there but me and the workmen, until I heard someone ask in my ear, "You like this work?" and saw the older Signor Toso was standing beside me.

"*Bello, bello,*" was the best I could do in Italian for such beauty. Pointing to the workman with the tools I asked, "The master?"

"*Si, si,*" Signor Toso answered.

The man with the poker stepped back, so did the master. The workman holding the giant tongs suddenly rolled them and the mass within, in sweeping circles around his head, and we saw the mass swell and bulge as if a bellows were blowing it from within. He stopped as suddenly as he had begun. He set the tongs on the master's bench, opened and drew them slowly away. And there on the bench was a Venetian glass bowl of amethyst color with a fluted handle on either side, delicate as a cobweb and as symmetrical as if it had been produced with precision instruments. But I had seen it produced by the hands of an artisan.

I hadn't noticed a large vat standing nearer the center furnaces until I saw couriers of the master dip into it the ends of their pokers, now empty of glass. Steam rose from the vat and I realized it was filled with water and that the workmen were quenching the heat from their pokers. They stood around the master looking at his creation. They leaned on their pokers as if they were leaning on staffs, and they talked among themselves nodding at the bowl. One of the workmen younger than the others rested his staff against the bench. I watched him go to a far corner of the room. In the dimness, I could barely make out, he was standing in front of a keg, I thought. I was right. He turned back carrying a pitcher filled with red wine. He handed this to the master who drank first, and then passed it around among his workmen.

That was a moment to remember. I had seen the performance of an artist and the recognition given to him and his accomplishment.

Signor Toso left me, went over to the master and added his words of approbation, nodding and pointing to the beautiful bowl. He returned to me with a paper in his hand. I had seen it thumbtacked to the side of the table on which the bowl stood. Signor Toso showed it to me. It was a sketch in the colors of the bowl.

Mr. Nutting joined us and looked over my shoulder at the drawing. "Can you beat it?" he said and shook his head. "I never saw anything like it."

He wanted Signor Toso to understand. "I am an engineer," he

said pointing to himself. And to Signor Toso, "You know that word?"

Signor Toso nodded. "*Si,*" he said, "engineer. *Si, si.*"

Mr. Nutting added to me, "My whole training was that. I took my degree in it. Merchandising is the last thing I thought I'd get into."

He resumed slowly with Signor Toso. "I know instruments, machinery," he continued. "I know how to make things with machinery," he repeated.

Signor Toso nodded and answered, "Machinery is good for railroads, automobiles. Not for glass. For glass it is a man; father, son; father, son. You understand?"

Mr. Nutting nodded helplessly. "Yes," he said wearily, "I understand," and turning to me again, "but I'll never get him to understand what I mean. Look at that sketch. The only measurements that fellow took were with a compass like school kids use. I was watching him every step of the way. He just looked at it from time to time and then went on modeling. And the speed! Did you see what they were working with? I bet those were the same tools they were using in the thirteenth century. Have you seen how they get their colors?"

I said I'd been too preoccupied with what was going on in front of me.

"Well," Mr. Nutting elaborated, "I saw some youngsters carrying ground-up paint in old iron vessels, shallow and all out of shape. I know they're all hundreds of years old. And I'll be darned if one of those men didn't throw some of it into a big pot exactly like a pinch of salt into water you were going to cook vegetables in. And just look at what comes out!"

He broke off suddenly. "My gosh," he exclaimed, "I haven't taken a single picture. I never had that happen before. I was just so darn fascinated, I guess.

He hurried off, stopped suddenly, and came back with the suggestion that he take my camera, attach his flashlight equipment to it and alternately use mine and his machine, so that I would have my own record.

I was grateful since, as I told him, I not only didn't own flash-light equipment, I couldn't possibly manipulate it.

While he worked I continued my conversation with Signor Toso. Sophy and Zella joined me, each babbling an excited report of having edged away from the spot where they had been sta-tioned, and skirting carefully the darting pokers, had seen other things in the making. "Fabulous," each insisted, "mine is the most beautiful you ever saw. You must come and see it."

Signor Toso caught the gist of all this, smiled, and nodded his head repeatedly. "You like it," he said beaming, "you like it."

Every minute or two I would see something I had not noticed before. Now I called his attention to an adjoining room, smaller than the one in which we stood, but with furnaces in the center. My eye had been caught by movement there, and I saw that young boys, very young, some of them looking not more than ten or eleven years old, were moving about with pokers, carrying hives of glass to older boys at benches and tables like the ones in our room. I asked who they were and what they were doing.

"Apprentices," Signor Toso answered, and half in Italian, half English, made us understand that those were their furnaces and that when they had the time, they fashioned objects themselves, brought them to one of the masters in the big room for criticism. If the master approved a piece it was included in the stock to be sold, and that of course made the apprentice very proud.

I think I must have looked idiotically open-mouthed. Racing through my mind was the realization that from just such a studio came pictures that today carry the notation "School of Titian," et cetera. I was as good as being in the fifteenth century standing where I was, but that is not easy to explain in Italian, and further-more, Signor Toso could have felt no such incongruity.

Walter Luscher took us to a little restaurant for lunch not far from the factory and along the quais. We ate in a garden and had as additional company three handsome cats. We were the only guests and were welcomed gracefully by the proprietor and his wife, who, at our arrival, had been hanging up the wash at the far end of the garden and came toward us wiping her hands on a bright checked apron. Sitting at a long wooden table we had a view of the backs of the buildings that lined the quais, evidently they were dwellings with gardens below like the one in which we sat. Outside many of the windows hung a little wooden cage in which a bird trilled. The proprietress offered us a choice of omelet or fresh fish, with restrictions. Omelet, she said, was not a meal for a man, it lacked vigor; men should have fish, ladies could have omelet.

The men were a little rueful over this allotment, protesting wistfully they preferred an omelet, but she was inflexible. They had fish and the proprietor brought a bottle of white wine. The cats joined us when the fish were served. I think they were the reason we had not been permitted omelet all around, because vocally and with paws tapping the legs of the gentlemen, they made very evident their expectancy of sharing the fish, and they were not disappointed.

The sun came out as we ate, and the day was warm. We reviewed the morning, savoring it again. Mrs. Nutting and Walter Luscher had explored more of the factory than any of the rest of us. I had traveled the least, rooted to one spot, they all declared, every time they had looked at me.

"That's the kind of sight-seer I find I am," I told them. "I'm no ground-coverer. When I see something that interests me, that's where I stay."

On the way back to the launch we repassed the Communist posters that had startled us so on our arrival. They seemed to me even stranger now when we had spent most of the hours between in the fifteenth century. There was scarcely a workman, Signor Toso had said, in his employ who did not share his own length of lineage of glass blowers, father to son.

We were back in Venice at the Danieli about four o'clock. I may have stood in one spot most of the morning, I told my friends, but I was now going exploring and I would thank them not to accompany me. They assured me this would give them no sense of deprivation, and I left them.

I thought as I walked along how comfortable it was to be with old friends. People had said to me, and undoubtedly to them before we left, what a risky undertaking this was, three women starting out on a trip together to be joined by a fourth and eventually in London by even a fifth. Two women traveling together were generally at outs with each other before the trip was well under way. What would it be with such a number? Feuds and gangings-up, taking sides; probably not one of us would be speaking to any other member of the group by the time the trip was over.

We had considered the possibility of this, talking it over among ourselves one night in New York, and had come to the conclusion that the chances of survival were greater by the very reason of the number of us. Two people were too interdependent. We had reached an age when each of us needed and demanded time by herself. We had long since passed the schoolgirl age of traveling four abreast, arms around one another's waist. But, equally, with this number not one of us needed to go by herself if she wished companionship. She need feel neither abandoned nor surfeited, and the groupings could shift. Our number made that flexible, too. Already this was the way it was working out. Zella and Sophy were perhaps doing some sight-seeing together, perhaps separately writing letters. I didn't know, I didn't have to care. I was a contented traveler.

I came to a shop just off St. Mark's Square that displayed in its window Olivetti portable typewriters. At home I had heard of these typewriters, how light they were to carry, how easy to handle. I had had in mind the purchase of one in Rome. It startled me to see them here. Venice seemed such a strange environment for a typewriter. Had I thought of the Venice world of affairs, I would have pictured its business conducted in a fine Italian hand.

I went inside and was greeted by a beautiful young woman behind the counter. I asked if she spoke English, and she said apologetically it was not very good. If such a beauty, I thought, were in New York I doubted she would be selling typewriters for very long; her photograph modeling the most expensive clothes would be in every fashion magazine. She had lifted a typewriter to the top of a counter, removed it from its case and was explaining rapidly to me in charming English all its technical virtues. Since I know only enough about a typewriter to punch its keys, and even then only when I look, I gave her discourse little attention.

But when she had finished I said it sounded just what I wanted, and that I would purchase it. A look of dismay clouded her exquisite features. Surely I would not make the purchase now, she protested. I asked if some special permit were required. She did not understand this at first, but when she had grasped my question denied vigorously such a necessity. She must speak to the owner, she explained, to secure permission for a little adjustment in price to be made.

I am not so untraveled as to be ignorant of the bargaining that accompanies purchases abroad, but somehow I had supposed such maneuvering was for incidentals like dresses and pocketbooks. Mechanical things, I had assumed, would be on an inflexibly realistic basis. I was delighted to find this was not so. I love bargaining. I would come back, I promised, next day.

As I turned to go another young woman came through from the back of the shop. She carried a baby on her arm, was the sister of my saleslady, and we were introduced; the baby was her six months old son. We chatted a few minutes, I played with the baby who was adorable, learned a good deal of his sleeping and eating habits. They all three saw me on my way, the young man's arm propelled by his mother to a good-by wave.

I gave up any further exploring and returned to the hotel.

We dined that night at Ridotto's, recommended in a guidebook, and I cannot think why. The restaurant itself is bare of decoration with glaring white walls and overhead lights so bright that the other diners, like us, seemed to be squinting. The food was indifferent and so was the waiter.

An apéritif next day before lunch at Florian's was more to my liking than the cocktails had been at Harry's Bar. It is not so fashionable as it used to be but it has a kind of seedy dignity. I think it has charm.

Lunch at the Café Del Angelo was good but not spectacular. It is on a little street behind St. Mark's that is rather fun to find. A good many Germans were eating there. German and French tourists far outnumbered the Americans in Venice, and we were delighted to hear those languages as well as Italian around us. We had not come so far, we declared, in order to see and hear other Americans.

In the afternoon we hired a gondola and were photographed in it, giggling appropriately while this was done. Any tourist who feeds the pigeons in St. Mark's does not leave undone the other things that tourists should do. We stopped at the Ca'd'Oro, and when we found a crowd there and joined it to gape at an English motion picture company filming Romeo and Juliet, felt we were really in the tourist pattern.

Back at the hotel later in the afternoon I left my companions and went off on another solitary exploration. A particular delight in Venice, I think, is to take walks. In the first place, because at the outset it seems impossible with canals everywhere, and in the second place, because getting lost is inevitable and very pleasant. The streets are no wider than our sidewalks. They curve and turn bewilderingly. At the moment you are sure you are about to step back into St. Mark's, which is the sun from which all byways radiate, you find you have turned instead into a street you had

not seen before. And contrariwise, at the very instant you feel
totally lost you round a bend and are back at St. Mark's.

About five o'clock I rounded a bend and found myself outside
the typewriter shop. I went in, had delightful conversation with
my friends of the day before including the baby, and learned the
price of the typewriter had been reduced especially for me by two
dollars. I assured my saleslady and her sister my gratitude and
asked it be relayed to the proprietor, adding that I would take
the machine along. My friends were appalled. The sisters simultaneously exclaimed surely I could come back the following day.
They could now assure the proprietor my definite interest in the
machine and something more undoubtedly could be accomplished.
I told them I was leaving the following day and could give only
one more visit to this transaction. They were donwcast at this
news regretting that I was allotting such a brief time to this undertaking, but promised to achieve as much as was possible with only
another twenty-four hours in which to work. And again I was
waved off from the threshold.

We dined that night at our hotel, our only meal there since the
first day's lunch, except for breakfast each morning in our own
apartment. We found the terrace jammed and were unable to get
a table before nine-thirty. We had dressed for dinner and were
glad we had. Everyone dining there was in evening clothes. The
food was excellent.

After dinner we took a brief stroll to St. Mark's and back,
without incident. Sophy seemed a little downcast. We had liqueurs
at the hotel but I didn't bump into any American, not even the
Nuttings. The Nuttings had left for Rome that morning.

The following was our last day in Venice.

In the morning Sophy and Zella went to see the Lido, by boat
of course. I stayed behind because I had more important things
to do. Mission typewriter was to be accomplished at half-past ten.
But first I went to the address on my receipt to collect the finished
prints of the photographs that had been taken of us the day before

in the gondola. The photographer's studio was perhaps two minutes' walk from St. Mark's Square and I reached it in a little over
half an hour. The streets I walked and that turned out to be not
the ones indicated on my receipt, were charming and totally unfamiliar, though I thought I had covered that entire area on
previous promenades. It made a pleasant excursion.

A good many other tourists were waiting for their photographs
when I finally arrived at the proper place. The last obstacle had
been three very steep flights of stairs. I was wheezing audibly
when I crossed the threshold; so, I noticed immediately, were
some of the others, evidently recent arrivals. We smiled at one
another understandingly and one customer rose from the only chair
in the room, offering it to me.

There were certainly ten of us in a space not much bigger than
the average bathroom at home. Conversation was in French and
German. Another customer wheezed in and I relinquished my
chair. It was a kind of "Going to Jerusalem" in reverse. No one
in the group seemed to belong to the establishment, but presently
a young man bustled between bead portieres across a doorway,
carrying a considerable pile of envelopes. He was at the far end of
the room.

He pushed his way through us to a table in a corner. He put
his pile of envelopes down on it, patted them and looked inquiringly from one to the other of us. We handed him our respective receipts, those of us the farthest away passing them on
from neighbor to neighbor. The young man sorted through his
pile, found the envelope that matched the receipt number and
delivered it. Immediately he received it, each customer opened his
and took out the photographs. Everyone was interested so there
was a general distribution and it took a little time to reassemble
the sets. Payment was somewhat involved, too, due to lack of
space and the fact that the young photographer had no change.
But in the group we made change for one another.

Later in the day when I showed the photographs to Zella and
Sophy, I found my set included a shot of a smiling stout German

couple and recognized the woman as the one who had given me her chair.

I went on to the typewriter shop, and found waiting there the two sisters, the baby, the baby's grandmother and her son, the younger brother of the two girls. We were introduced immediately and shook hands all around, my financial intermediary acting as interpreter and explaining to me that Mama and Luigi had come to offer me felicitations on the purchase of the beautiful little machine and congratulations on the news I was about to receive. My saleslady paused dramatically. Everyone watched me, their eyes shining.

A further adjustment had been made, she announced, and smiled modestly at such achievement. Because of the friendship Italy felt for America and pride that an Italian machine was going to be taken to New York, from the price for which this machine was always sold, five dollars was to be removed. She flung out her arm and opened her hand wide. It was beautiful, as if we all saw the five dollars floating through the open door. No one could speak for a moment, then Mama gave a deep sigh—"Aaaah," she said.

I followed with, *"Grazie, grazie, grazie,"* and we shook hands all around, the baby's hand put by his mother into mine.

As I was counting out the money, Mama requested our interpreter to ask if I were a secretary to an American millionaire. I understood, however, and by putting *scribo* and *libro* together, and adding an inspiring pantomime of myself at a microphone, conveyed to these charming and astute people that I wrote books and talked on the radio. The ahs and sighs that followed this announcement could have blown that five dollars all the way to the farthest canal. I was requested to shake hands all around again, and I shook the hand of each, including the baby.

I thought I could make my exit on this, but I was mistaken. The typewriter I had been shown was not the one I was allowed to take. A fresh one was brought from the storeroom, unpacked from its outer carton, removed from its carrying case, turned on the counter toward me with the request that I try it to make sure the action suited me. If not, another would be brought out.

In some embarrassment from the unblinking attention of the family, I typed out, "Now is the time for all good men to come to the aid of the party," and pronounced the machine exactly to my liking.

Mama asked if I would be so gracious as to autograph the sentiment I had just expressed and allow her to keep it as a memento from an American writer. I have never before wittingly appropriated someone else's prose, but I left with Mama that sentence as my own creation, and I hope I may be forgiven for it. Daughter, I knew, was not going to have an easy time translating it for Mama. I hoped they would think of me as a writer of profound and abstruse philosophy.

The need to leave, I felt, was urgent and I expressed this. The news was greeted by little cries of regret, but understanding. The typewriter was snapped back into its carrying case, and I had got as far as the door when young brother opening it for me told us it was starting to rain. This announcement provoked a little drama and considerable delay. It was not to be considered, Mama declared, that I should go out into the rain. My clothes, my beautiful new machine; all, all would be ruined. I endeavored to explain the alternative of my missing the train to Milan, and Mama gave in on condition that her son, provided with an umbrella, would accompany me back to the hotel. The umbrella was produced from a back room. I shook hands all around once more, baby included, and the last I saw of the family as I set off was baby's arm propelled in a farewell salute.

Back at the hotel with the luggage brought down ready for our departure, I sat in the salon to wait for Sophy's and Zella's return. I noticed three middle-aged women like me sitting a few feet away from my chair. Two of them were in a position that indicates fatigue and middle age, feet flat on the floor, knees wide apart, heads forward. The third, however, sat briskly erect, one knee crossed over the other.

One of them spoke, and it was evident she was American and from the South. "When I see that Statue of Liberty, I'm going to say to her, 'Don't you ever let me get on the ocean out of sight of you again as long as I live. I don't want to be a fool twice.' "

The other dejected one raised her head a little. "Well, Ella," she said, "you must admit it's been beautiful."

"I admit the beauty," was Ella's answer, "Lord knows I'm fairly drenched with it, but I don't understand why beauty has to smell so terrible. And furthermore, I don't know why you can't have beauty and food that's fit to eat. I haven't had a mouthful since I came that I'd give to a dog back home. Why didn't I have the sense to stay there? Don't let anybody say 'travel' to me again."

The third one interrupted. I had a feeling she was going to try to bring a little sunshine, and she did. "Ella," she said brightly, "did I tell you the cute thing my little granddaughter said in a letter I got from my daughter this morning?"

Ella regarded her dourly. "No, Mary," she said, "you did not, and I appreciate that very much."

I saw Zella and Sophy standing in the doorway and went joyfully to meet them.

Chapter 8

IN THE Venice railway station Sophy confided to Zella and me that ever since our wait in Milan on our way to Venice three days before, she had been remembering wistfully the sandwiches and Chianti she had seen other passengers purchasing there for breakfast. She asked wistfully if Zella and I would be agreeable to buying the same provisions here and make them our lunch in the train instead of going to the restaurant car. Zella and I were receptive to the idea and we boarded the train each carrying a large brown paper bag and Sophy, in addition, tucked under her arm a large bottle of Chianti and a package of paper cups. The sandwiches were thin slices of ham in a narrow roll about eight inches long with crisp golden crust.

We counted the meal a delightful picnic, the other occupant of our compartment, a stylish Italian lady, obviously counted us a raffish lower-class lot and her unwilling proximity to it, regrettable. After her haughty refusal of a paper cup of Chianti, we made no further companionable overtures.

At a quarter to five we were walking through the railroad station in Milan we had seen from the windows of our train three days before, and just outside we found a bus marked "Palace Hotel" which was our objective. The bus was a surprise and we were grateful for it, because by now, what with my typewriter and a few odd pieces I had purchased to accommodate the souvenirs I was already accumulating, our luggage totaled thirteen items. It was on the pavement by the bus as the baggage was being loaded that Zella introduced her theme song, with which she obliged without request for a run of thirty days, closing only with the last rendering at the customs desk at Idlewild Field, New York on June 7. The song began, "We have a total of thirteen [this number increased] bags." And the chorus that we learned in no time and joined in ran, "But only three are mine."

The Palace Hotel is new, built since the last war, and very comfortable. Our suite included in addition to two bedrooms and large bath, a hallway large enough to include our luggage, and a balcony outside one of the rooms. It also included more gadgets than I, in my simple walk of life, had ever encountered. But I discovered these gradually and disconcertingly. We took no time on our arrival for such investigations.

The instant our baggage was delivered to us we left the hotel for a walk. I can report nothing of whatever places of interest there may be between the Palace Hotel and the Cathedral of Milan, but I can set down with underlining that the traffic at five-thirty in that section of Milan makes the cars on Madison Avenue at that hour a sedate procession taking their occupants to church. Five minutes after we had begun our walk there was no hunger left in me for the beauty of the Milan Cathedral. The only thing that drove me on to see it was the impossibility of turning back to the safety of the Palace Hotel, though I longed to take refuge there. On the sidewalk pedestrians whirled us halfway around and others back again as if the three of us were "it" in Blind Man's Buff. On the curb the pedals of passing bicycles nicked our shins, and in the streets to which we were pushed from the rear, motorists played "one, two, three, and down goes she" with the three of us. I suppose Italian cars have brakes, unless as a measure of postwar economy they are omitted as foolish luxuries. But I venture to wager if they are still included in the equipment

of an automobile, a used car is turned in with the brake as fresh as
the day it left the factory. The horn and the accelerator get the
hardest wear.

At one crossing, Sophy, Zella and I scattered like leaves before
an autumn wind. I came to rest in a little haven between two
parked cars, and I sat down on the bumper of one because my
knees were chattering. From my retreat I peeked out cautiously
dreading the possible sight of my friends, or parts of them, scattered about the street. Mercifully there was no evidence of such
dissolution, but I saw an Italian traffic policeman, and that *is* a
pretty sight. I don't know where these officers receive their training; from the Sadler's Wells Ballet School, I should think. Beyond the first one I spotted I caught sight of a fellow officer on
a near-by intersection giving a duplicate performance.

A "stop" was indicated by the left hand smacked smartly
against the thigh; the right hand straight ahead in the manner of
a duelist's thrust, except with the hand up, palm out. Permission
for traffic from the right to advance was indicated by first the
left arm above the head, palm out. That halted traffic from the
left. Then with the right arm softly curved, in the kind of sweeping motion I used to make when, playing jacks, I executed the
maneuver called "pigs in a pen," he coaxed toward him the traffic
on his right. To stop the traffic on either side in order to allow
intersecting lines to cross, this artist crossed arms over his breast,
and then as if on an inner count of two, extended his arms,
at either side with palm out and with drama in every widespread
finger. I was sorry to see no leaping nor twinkle-toes. Perhaps foot-
work is postgraduate study.

What I did see, however, were my friends safe on a sidewalk,
but running up and down it, evidently searching for me. Their
concern forced me from my sanctuary. I ventured out, and in a
series of the sort of leaps I had hoped to see the policeman make,
I reached my dear ones, and we shook hands all around in mutual

congratulations and thanksgiving that, though nervously impaired, we were physically intact.

By the grace of God and the city planners, there were no more streets to cross in order to reach the cathedral. Instead we walked through the astonishing Galleria Vittorio Emanuele. This is an arcade under a glassed roof, but of such vast proportion it takes on the aspect of a little city under glass. There are restaurants, night clubs, shops of every sort. We were particularly drawn to mouth-watering delectables in the windows of pastry shops. There are theater ticket agencies, travel offices, banks. The space for pedestrians between the lines of buildings is as wide as a boulevard; and over all of this the glass roof.

We emerged from the little city and saw the cathedral. We had one narrow thoroughfare to cross before we were actually at its door, but the crossing was so simple by comparison with those we had previously breasted, we scarcely counted it a street at all; no more than crossing Madison Avenue against the lights.

Let architects and art critics snub the Milan Cathedral as they do, deploring its ornateness. I think it is magnificent; a combination of grandeur and delicacy.

We were given very little time in its cool, vast interior, because the doormen, or whatever one calls those officials in churches who function in that capacity, were closing up for the night. As we came out we saw, on the square that the cathedral faces, a violent political meeting in progress, so violent that in addition to the over-all shouting, there were several fist fights going on among individuals around the fringe. We scuttled back to the Galleria. Zella said its glass roof made her feel "*sous cloche*," like breast of guinea hen.

We sat down at a little table outside the Restaurant Biffi and ordered Cinzano while we watched the mass of people going by, some hurrying, others strolling; men in black business suits, the women almost without exception in well-tailored suits and, with no exception, bareheaded. I do not remember seeing a hat on any woman in Milan. We saw a number of charming rendezvous and nudged one another, grinning with silly pleasure.

At half-past six, it turned very chilly and we debated going back to the hotel, but the interior of Biffi's, the restaurant proper, would be a more amusing place, we decided, and I volunteered to return to the hotel for warm coats. Zella was proving to be the one of the three of us to leap first into voluntary service, but this time Sophy overruled her.

"Now listen, pack horse," she said, "let Emily do it. She's the drone of this group. I do the banking, you're always running errands, counting the luggage. I know, I know," she added hastily, "you have only three bags. But just relax for a change. I'm all for Emily waiting on us."

Zella subsided reluctantly and I departed, observing as I left that I was only too happy to be of assistance if either of them would point out a field in which they considered me competent.

Sophy called after me, "Taking a taxi, maybe?"

She was mistaken about this suggestion. I was not competent in a taxi. And I was very nearly deranged by the time I reached the Palace Hotel. I had no difficulty getting a taxi. There was a line of them outside the Galleria. Had I known how it was going to be riding in one I would have elected to court death by walking not only the crossings again but right down the middle of those streets.

A week later a friend in Rome gave me an explanation of why Italian taxi drivers behave as they do. "It's the Italian temperament," she said, "to want to be in the middle of whatever is going on. When a driver comes to a corner, he's impatient to know what may be happening out of sight, so he presses on to reach the middle of the intersection where he can look both ways. Since the drivers on the intersection feel the same way, obviously the middle of the intersection is where they meet. And of course when trolleys, buses and pedestrians are converging, that is sheer intoxication to a driver. That's when he really presses down on the accelerator."

That's exactly what my taxi driver did, press down on the accelerator. The slam of the door as I got in the cab was to him like the raising of the barrier at Epsom Downs. We were off, sometimes on four wheels, sometimes on two as we rounded corners; his foot on the accelerator, hand on the horn. For the first block or so, I was too frozen with fright to be able to make a sound. I couldn't have moved of my own volition, but I was moving, bobbing from side to side, and slithering back and forth across the back seat. There wasn't so much as an inside handle to clutch as a stabilizer.

But there came a moment when the need for speech thawed the deep freeze I'd been in. I found I could talk, only I didn't know what to say. "The hat is on the chair. The pen on the table is not a black pen, it is a brown pen," I could have told the driver in Italian, but as expressions of what was in my mind, they were misleading.

"Do you speak English?" I shouted.

"No, Signora," he called back, and laughed gaily.

I considered his remark as unfunny as any I have ever heard, but I was unable to say that, either.

As we rounded a circle like a shot-put before it is released, some Italian words came to me from study of the piano from the age of six to fourteen. I threw them at the maniac in front of me behind the wheel. "*Non fortissimo,*" I yelled. "*Troppo forte, piano, legato, diminuendo, pianissimo. Tempo troppe vivace.*" I could feel no change, however, in our tempo. My eyes were shut in order to pray more fervently, and not to see. But I heard my driver say, "*Ah, si, si, si, Signora.*"

I opened my eyes and leaned forward to press through this opening I had made in the sound barrier between us.

He had both hands off the wheel, crossed over his breast, "*Si, si, si,*" he repeated. "*Opera, La Scala, Milano. Molto bello, molto bello.*"

He stopped the car with the vigor on the brake he had applied to the accelerator. I was leaning forward, my mouth was open, I was toppled over with violence by the jar and very nearly bit his ear.

From the porter at the hotel I learned one of the few musical terms I didn't think would have been the magic word. "*Adagio*" with "*per favore*" added for politeness. I used it in another taxi on the return to Biffi's. I can't say I achieved tranquillity from it but at least I was able to stay in one corner.

I found my friends inside the restaurant and the great arcade almost entirely deserted. They said it had happened almost in an instant; one minute crowded, the next minute with scarcely a passerby. Our dinner was excellent.

We had planned to go on to Rome the following morning after a visit to the Last Supper. But we learned from a bulletin at the desk that there was to be the following night a performance at La Scala of *Adriana Lecouvreur*. It was an opera none of us had heard nor cared particularly about, but to miss an opportunity of seeing any opera at La Scala seemed to us little less than idiotic. We ordered tickets and extended our hotel reservations.

That night I investigated a provocative row of push buttons beside my bed. Some of these were labeled as is customary in many hotels: Valet—Waiter—Maid—et cetera. I tried those that were unlabeled. One, I discovered, turned out the ceiling light in the bedroom, another turned out the one in our hallway, and a third shot a bolt locking our outside door. Very handy devices I considered them when one has forgotten to do those things before getting into bed.

At breakfast the next morning we decided to hire a car and drive to the Villa d'Este at Lake Como, going first to see the Last Supper. With the day organized—and next to good wine and food, Sophy likes to contemplate a well-organized day—we hurried into our clothes. As I was toweling after my bath, over the tub I noticed a gadget I had not observed while I was in it. The contrivance was a very thick rope, silk-covered like an old-fashioned bell pull, and it reached from the ceiling almost to the level of the tub. I am accustomed to bath towels of regulation size. They allow me to play a brisk back-and-forth rubbing motion from shoulders down. A European bath towel is a bath sheet. Enveloped in one of these I become like a figure from the Laocoön group. I cannot even extricate my hands to achieve briskness with them. But as I wrestled in and out of the Palace Hotel sheet, I gave what attention I could spare to the rope and came to the decision that it was there to assist a bather out of the tub. Instead of heaving up from a grip on the hot and cold water taps, he could rise nimbly by gripping the rope. I approved such ingenuity and resolved to try it for myself the next morning, regretting that in my haste I had overlooked it on this round, and would therefore be able to benefit from it only once.

The car we had ordered was waiting at the door when we came downstairs, the chauffeur smartly turned out in a long white linen duster with dark blue collar. Sophy asked him in Italian and with superfluous wordage, it seemed to me, to take us to the convent of the Church of Santa Maria della Grazie that holds the Last Supper.

"Showoff," I muttered and added succinctly and clearly, "*Adagio, per favore.*"

No one else was in the room when we looked at the Da Vinci picture, though I had understood from a guidebook that the place is generally crowded with visitors. It is strange that the wall on which this picture is painted is the only one of that room that withstood bombing. The other walls have been rebuilt now, but there is still much finishing work to be done. The picture itself, though badly faded, had to me the arresting dramatic quality I had anticipated to find there; no need of strong bright colors to convey it. Zella pointed out that scattered on the table in front of the figures were rolls exactly like those we had bought at the railway station in Venice the day before.

We were at Lake Como by noon and had an apéritif on the hotel terrace above the bright blue water. Though the day was sunny it was chilly enough to warrant our keeping on our top-coats. We lunched outside, however, and a gentleman at the next table, seeing my camera, obligingly offered to photograph the three of us. I took more pictures after lunch of the garden and the view of the mountains across the lake. When we had walked for half an hour or so we were ready to go back. I felt about Lake Como as the man from Boston said of another beauty spot. "It's lovely to look at, but when I travel abroad I want something more than that. I like to go to places I can get my teeth into."

Accordingly we stopped in the city proper of Como and sank our teeth satisfyingly into the cathedral there, because in addition to our pleasure in the edifice itself, we found charm in the activity going on inside. A visit was anticipated the following day from a cardinal, we discovered, and this had set up a fine flurry of dusting and cleaning. The organist was practicing, men in smocks were placing in holders candles at least six feet high, while other workers below gave directions for making them straight and symmetrical to a hairsbreadth.

We were home in good time to dress for the opera and we dined on the roof of the hotel. We discovered only at the opera itself, to our dismay, that the seats the hotel porter had been able to secure were in the last row of the top balcony. Zella and Sophy reconciled themselves to this, but I am not so docile. I couldn't see anything. I repeated this several times to my friends, together with perhaps unnecessary but to me important information that I was dressed for downstairs and that was where I wished to be.

At the first intermission I persuaded my companions to accompany me all the way below in the hope that I might find some way of bettering our position. Zella was amenable to going or staying, she is a most adaptable human being. Sophy found it difficult, she said, to decide whether the inevitable climb back up the stairs would be more trying than listening to my complaints the remainder of the evening. She decided to risk the climb.

Working my way through the crowd in the foyer I found among the ushers an old rather frail man. Hoping his years had mellowed him I said to him yearningly, and in English with Italian word endings, that we were strangers, Americans in Milan for the first time; all our lives we had wanted to come to this great opera the La Scala. Now we were here but our seats were at the very top, and I pointed heavenward. It was a tragedy.

The old gentleman was moved, I could see that, and I signaled my friends to join me. There was not a seat in the house unoccupied, he said sadly, but he would be happy to show us during what remained of the intermission, the museum connected with the opera house. He led the way and we followed him through a series of exquisite salons, each containing mementos of great composers and artists who had sung there. I was looking at the manuscript of Verdi's "Requiem" when the signal came that the intermission was ended.

I turned immediately to our guide, thanked him deeply for his kindness and then, "Must we go way back up there?" I quavered.

There was a pause. Zella, Sophy and I waited anxiously.

"Come," the old man said.

He led us back through the lovely rooms, then on into the auditorium itself. He drew aside a heavy velvet curtain and we found ourselves in a sort of foyer at the back of the house enclosed with heavy curtains, but open toward the stage. This was behind the last row. He indicated we must stand, but we could remain there. I assured him in a whisper our happiness at being there, and our willingness to forego sitting down.

The lights were down, the curtain rose on the second act of the opera. Therefore, it was not until the next intermission that we saw the interior itself. It is completely satisfying, all white and gold and rich red brocade, just what an opera house should be. Zella pointed out a clock which neither Sophy nor I had noticed. It was

set just above the stage in the proscenium arch and Zella told us
it had an illuminated dial so that all during the performance one
could if one liked see exactly what time it was. Zella wondered
why one wanted to know that the tenor aria was being delivered at
precisely ten twenty-three, or whatever.

We went again into the grand foyer, and this time took note
of the other members of the audience. The women were mag-
nificently dressed in full and very elaborate evening clothes. Most
of the men were in dinner clothes, a few in business suits. By the
last act we were leg-weary; Sophy and Zella were making pointed
remarks about the pleasure of sitting, whether down or upstairs.
We saw by the clock that the opera ended at twelve-fifteen. It had
begun at nine. We had stood all but twenty minutes or so of that
time, and we fell into bed exhausted.

Next morning lying in my tub I saw the rope dangling just above
me, and remembered that the day before I had worked out in
my mind its purpose. I promptly put it to the test and was highly
gratified by the ease with which, by pulling, I soared up.

While I was wrestling with the bath sheet around me, a man
appeared in the open doorway to the bathroom and bowed.

"*Buon giorno, Signora,*" he said smiling.

I got both arms inside the bath sheet and stared at my caller, too
dumbfounded to answer his greeting.

From behind his back he brought forward a menu and extended
it to me.

I shook my head. I dared not risk letting go the bath sheet, even
with one hand, and besides I didn't know what the menu was for.

My visitor nodded his head. "Ah," he said, "not fruit with the
breakfast, only the regular coffee, rolls with hot milk?"

I found my voice but it was a little shrill. "Yes," I told him, "I
want that breakfast. But not now. What are you doing here?" I
added, and by this time I was outraged.

The waiter looked astonished. "But the Signora has rung for
breakfast," he said at last.

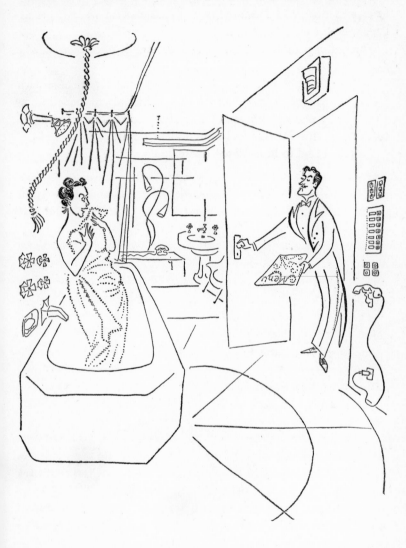

I understood this in Italian and was exasperated. I had no Italian to express this but I indicated how preposterous it was for me to have rung for breakfast there.

The waiter pointed to the rope above the tub. "The Signora has rung," he repeated.

How he had got in the outside door I do not know, unless by pulling on the rope I had unlocked that as well as summoned him. I had at the moment no pantomime at my command with which to ascertain this. Neither had I any Italian words.

"Well," I said to him, "forevermore."

Chapter 9

THE RAPIDO is the de luxe train to Rome. All seats on it are reserved and they are delivered to the passenger in something the manner of bestowing an award. The three grannies were not impressed. We judged it the only uncomfortable train in which we traveled abroad. Instead of a division into compartments the cars are open like our day coaches at home only not so roomy. On one side of the aisle the seats are single, on the other, not only double, but in facing pairs.

Happily the fourth occupant of our double pair was a charming woman from Milan on her way to see her boy in boarding school in Florence. She spoke beautiful English and told us she had a daughter at school in England. She talked interestingly about young people in Italy. The girls, she said, of good families wanted the independence that having a job or a career would bring, but were as yet given little or no opportunity to hold other than subordinate positions, with a few outstanding exceptions. The general pattern was, as she described it, very much as I had known it in America twenty-five years ago. Her own daughter, she admitted, would probably stay on in England after her education was completed because she had found greater opportunity there in pursuing the career she had chosen. Many Italian girls were doing the same thing.

Lunch was served to us at our seats on individual trays. The food was excellent and so was the service.

We waved our traveling companion off the train at Florence, craning our necks out the window with open curiosity until we saw her greeted by a very handsome boy. We beamed happily at the sight of this reunion, and then as the train pulled out of the station, admitted to one another we had certainly marked ourselves as grandmothers. It was Sophy who pointed out to us the mark of the grandmother. Time was, she said, when every one of us would have been agog in the hope of discovering that the woman was having a secret rendezvous with a lover. But not now. There we were, the three of us grinning contentedly at such a nice-looking boy coming to greet his mother. This was not a cheering thought. We took to our books and there was no further conversation.

At the Hotel Eden in Rome, the clerk at the desk told us a Signora Newbold had at that very instant been shown to her room. She was at the moment ascending in the elevator. She had just arrived and had been inquiring for Signora Jacobs and party.

"Margie's here," we said in chorus, and hurried after her.

We were calling happy greetings when we came to the door of Margie's room, but we stopped at the threshold. The door was open but the room was too crowded for us to enter. Three porters were unloading luggage from their backs and from a small cart, and Margie, in a curious language that sounded like French with Italian endings interlaced with American idiom, was directing its disposal.

Zella suggested it might be a good idea for her and me to find the room that we were to occupy, and leave Sophy to discover if in that room she was to share with her sister there would be space for her and her own luggage that was at the moment on the way up from downstairs. Zella further volunteered to change places with Sophy and move in with Margie. "After all," she began, "even with our thirteen pieces . . ."

Sophy and I came in on cue, "You have only three."

"That's just what I was going to say," Zella added.

Sophy was grateful for Zella's offer, but declined it. Her verdict was that a sister had more chance than a friend of achieving elbow room, because after all in families no holds were barred.

Zella and I went on to our own room, waited there for our luggage, made our own little adjustment of my seven pieces and her three, and rejoined the sisters. We found them chattering happily and the room sufficiently cleared to allow an aisle from door to the beds, on which the four of us sat. I pointed out with some satisfaction that both this arrangement and spirit were more compatible with the boarding school age than with a grandmother's, and that there was no necessity for us to consider ourselves so inflexibly shelved as Sophy had indicated at the station in Florence.

We were delighted to see Margie and she, in turn, so happy to find us she was, she said, fairly giddy with pleasure and relief. All the way over on the boat she had been haunted by the recurrent conviction she had voiced during the planning of the trip, that she would have to pursue us from town to town in Italy because we would not have waited for her. She felt sorry, she said, for a man who had met her boat at Naples that day, at the instigation of the travel agency that had booked her passage. The man was earnest, conscientious and slow. While he was telling her about the accommodations he had in the hotel at Naples so that she might pass the night comfortably there and set out for Rome the following day, she was hurtling past him, shouting to all within hearing distance a request to be shown how to get the train for Rome immediately. He had followed, continuing his explanation of the room waiting for her and the careful planning of the travel agency. He was still explaining this to her from the station platform, she said, as her train pulled out.

It was obvious that Margie had a bad cold. When I pointed this out to her saying I was sorry, she rounded on me with an indignant denial and simultaneously a request to me not to talk about it. I told her I hadn't intended making it the subject of a thesis.

Margie explained her vehemence. Agnes, a sister left at home, had telephoned from Philadelphia to Margie, five times during the crossing, in order to find out the condition of Margie's cold and report they were all fine at home. Each time the call came, Margie had been in the midst of a pleasant activity with a group of people. She had been forced to retire to her cabin and wait there for the connection to be made. This had taken anywhere from one to three hours. Under the best of circumstances she does not take kindly to confinement. This, forced upon her, had given her a particular dislike of her cold and a determination to ignore it.

However, when Sophy proposed we go out for some sight-seeing and waste no more time indoors, Margie begged us to give her time to change to a suit other than the one she was wearing. She wanted, she said, to get into a blue garbardine she had bought that would be the right weight for the weather, and if she took her mink stole, should it get any cooler, she would still be protected and her cold wouldn't get any worse.

We agreed to this without mentioning the word "cold."

When we came out on the street, Margie said it was warmer than she'd thought, and asked if we'd mind waiting while she took her mink stole back to the room because wearing it would certainly make her overheated and that was the worst thing that could happen when you had a cold. She went back into the hotel but returned almost immediately. She had decided, she said, that the best thing was to carry it. Carrying it was not after all like wearing it, but on the other hand if it should grow chilly by late afternoon, she would be equipped and not have to make us all come back, because the only thing she really cared about was making things easy for everybody.

We assured her of our appreciation of this noble purpose, and hailed a taxi to take us to the Colosseum.

A friend of mine once professed to being confused by my saying I have not a full enjoyment of anything unless I have seen it before. I do not find that opinion confusing. I know exactly what I mean by it. A sight that impresses me at all, overwhelms me at first viewing. It is only at the second and subsequent sights that I can emerge from this envelopment into enjoyment. In addition I have another kind of enjoyment that wells up from very deep inside me, and I am quite sure this is not special to me. There are probably very few people who do not experience it. It comes when I see for the first time something I have known about and of which I have seen reproductions during the greater part of my life, like the Winged Victory in the Louvre, Notre Dame, the canals and St. Mark's Square in Venice, the Last Supper in Milan, and on a Sunday afternoon in May and in Rome I saw for the first time the Colosseum.

The pictures and the stories all those years had been telling me how it would be, and that is exactly how it was, and I felt starting down deep in me the welling up of that special contentment. I hadn't known, however, that there would be a burst of wild flowers on the Palatine Hill; bright scarlet poppies and a yellow flower I didn't recognize. They were growing, too, in and around the Forum and we all approved that, preferring it, we said, to orderly care. I had never before seen an acanthus tree. They grow on the Palatine. I had never separated them from a Corinthian pillar. There are cypress trees, too, on the Palatine, and the sweet, heavy smell of orange blossoms is everywhere.

When we were too tired to climb or even walk farther we still could not bear to stop looking and voted to take a taxi to St. Peter's. At that instant of decision it became apparent to Sophy and me that Margie and Zella were going to compete for the "helpfulness to others" medal. Shouting simultaneously, "I'll get one," they sped ahead.

Zella's was the more conservative method. She halted at the curb and was content to raise her arm beckoning to all approaching vehicles. Margie's was as terrifying to see as the traffic itself. Plunging into the very heart of it, she darted from one car to another, inquiring on the run of the driver of each, "Taxi?" to the considerable astonishment of a good many gentlemen taking their families on a Sunday outing.

Sophy turned away, unable to bear the sight. But when Margie, unscathed, came up panting to urge us to follow her to an adjoining street where she declared the prospects looked brighter, Sophy had a taxi waiting, selected from a group at a taxi stand none of the rest of us had noticed. I gathered in Zella from the curb.

The taxi itself provided fresh opportunity for the medal candidates. The realization that one of us would have to sit on the little folding seat inspired them to a joyous struggle over which should be its occupant. While they were happily bumping heads and hips, Sophy went around to the other side, opened the door, lowered the seat and sat on it. But I had been the first one in and was comfortably settled in a corner of the back.

We came into St. Peter's while a service was taking place and were as gratified as if we had planned it that way. I like to remember that my first view is interlaced with the smell of incense, the sound of antiphonal choirs and the flash of the color of vestments as the procession passed me.

We had drinks before dinner at our own hotel. Margie was surprised and a little dismayed to see that we had taken to Cinzano with a twist of lemon peel, called Martini Vermouth. We had some difficulty each time we ordered, in assuring the bartender that even though Americans we did not wish Martini cocktails but Martini Vermouth with a twist of lemon. Margie expressed her sympathy to the bartender and her disappointment in us, after which she ordered a double Bourbon (very hard to get in Italy) in order, as she explained, to make the bartender feel better.

We dined at the Restaurant Capriccio, well recommended, but we found it only fair. It is a few blocks away from the Eden and footsore as we were we could not resist walking home in the soft cool air.

Monday morning we were in the Sistine Chapel at ten o'clock with several hundred other sight-seers. They made disconcerting company because there was no effort on the part of the guards to keep them quiet. The result was a babble of languages as guides conducted their flocks each in the language of the party; a German guide for a German group, a French guide for a French.

We almost turned back in our annoyance at this irreverent confusion, but were thankful later we had not done this because we were able to skirt the crowd, perch on a ledge against the wall, and looking above us at that ceiling, forget there was anyone else there.

From the chapel we went to the Vatican Museum and trudged some miles of corridors, as we looked at tapestries, illumined manuscripts, porcelain, glass, jewels, until, as the woman in Venice had said, we were drenched with treasures. We turned our backs on all of it and went home to lunch.

That afternoon Miss Anna Lea Lelli took us on a tour. She is a friend of Sophy's and had come to America representing Italy at an International Assembly of Women that met in New York in 1946. Herself an archeological and classical scholar, she is the daughter of a distinguished classicist, who, when the Pope was confined to the Vatican, expressed his displeasure by moving outside the gates of Rome and never setting foot in it again. But his daughter was not so aloof. She spent some little time detained in Rome by the Fascists, who found her activities not to their liking. Since the war Miss Lelli has applied her scholarship and knowledge of classical history to travelers who have the good fortune to know about her and seek her out. Her address is: 2 Via Lorenzo Magalotti, and her telephone number is 871310.

Sophy had been instrumental in bringing to America the European delegates to the International Assembly of Women, and in Philadelphia had entertained Miss Lelli and others of them. They had corresponded since that time and Sophy had written Miss Lelli we were coming. She was eager to show hospitality in return, and asked us to be her guests for the afternoon, regretting deeply she could not do more, because she was leaving the following morning to conduct a small group of people on a tour through France. All these things she reiterated as she gathered us up and led us to a magnificent car waiting at the Eden. The car and chauffeur, we learned, are part of her equipment as guide, and certainly this made sight-seeing very comfortable.

What followed was truly exciting. We stood on the hillside where we had wandered the afternoon before, while Miss Lelli, with the fervor and passion the true scholar knows, brought down the tribes from the surrounding hills into the valley below, traced the course of the streams that had brought water from those same hills to the valley and made a reason for that site to become the city of Rome. As we looked down on it she rebuilt the Forum for us. Of course I had heard these things before; the first time in Miss Boyce's class in ancient history at Miss Faulkner's School in Chicago. But sitting at a desk, textbook before me, is not like standing above the Forum, with a wind stirring the leaves of the acanthus trees, carrying to me the smell of orange blossoms and the voice of a Roman who had been in prison for love of her country and its history.

As we left the hill Miss Lelli urged us to keep in our minds the image of the Basilica across the way and carry it with us to the Pantheon. That was our next stop. She reminded us as we came up its steps that the Pantheon had become a church when Constantine turned Christian, and has been worshiped in ever since. The instant we crossed the threshold, she stopped talking. The music of Gounod's "Ave Maria" tumbled out from an organ somewhere. I have never been conscious of music filling completely a space, but here it was as if the music came from the dome itself. It was the music of the spheres, and it was also, we learned, part of Miss Lelli's plan for us. She had requested the organist to come that afternoon and, watching for our arrival, begin to play as we crossed the threshold.

"Now," Miss Lelli said when we had met and thanked the organist and been persuaded to go, "now," she said, "we go to St. Peter's, and you will remember how Michelangelo said when he created it, 'I shall take the base of the Basilica, place the dome of the Pantheon upon it, and reach to Heaven.' That is why I asked you to carry the image of the Basilica, and now you have the Pantheon to place upon it."

To see St. Peter's with her was no doubling back on the tracks we had placed there the day before. We had not seen Michelangelo's Pieta, and this above almost all other figures I would not have missed. I should not have known, however, had she not told us, that it was done when the artist was only twenty-four. Except for her guidance I should not have stood knowingly at the spot that marked the outer dimension Michelangelo himself had in-

tended as the boundary of St. Peter's, proportioning it so that the
dome should come slowly into view as one approaches the altar,
until it seems to be a moving sphere. There are a great many
travelers who know these things and many more, obviously more
than Miss Lelli was able to tell us in that one afternoon, but they
have not learned them from a more dedicated teacher.

For the most part I deplore my ignorance. That afternoon I
delighted in it, because I do not know of many experiences more
thrilling than having knowledge given to me generously and with
passionate love of it. There are few experiences also, I think, that
bring about such total exhaustion.

Miss Lelli had tea with us back at the hotel, but we were not
sorry to see her go. We had reached the saturation point. We did
not even go out to dinner. We ate at the hotel and went immediately to bed.

The Princess von Schwarzenburg is the wife of the Austrian
Ambassador to Rome, but Sophy and I had known her twenty
years before when she was Pussy de Spoelberch, and came from
her native Belgium with her brother to visit friends in Philadelphia.
She had not returned to America and I had not seen her in the
intervening years, but Sophy had visited her and had kept in touch
with her by letters. So knowing of this grandmothers' outing,
Pussy had telephoned asking to put a car at our disposal and
inviting us to lunch at the Austrian Embassy.

On the day following the pilgrimage with Miss Lelli, we gratefully accepted Pussy's offer of the car and were driven in it out to
the Villa d'Este at Tivoli. I knew we would find fountains there
but I had had no idea they would be in such acreage nor of such
beauty. In my opinion their glory is in no whit overwhelmed by
the splendor of the fountains at Versailles. I went into paroxysms
of picture taking, up and down the rows, snapping as fast as I
could turn the film. I was abashed to be caught by a group of
tourists taking several closeups of one that seemed to me to have
remarkable originality. This quaint conceit is a four-legged crea-

ture with wings, the upper part of the body a woman. It is lying as an animal rests, its forepaws extended, but from each of the woman's breasts the water flows in a vigorous, splendid stream. Finding a group of tourists at my elbow, I wished I might have been observed taking a more esthetic vista.

We went to the opera that night to see the first performance of a work by a Roman Senator. The opera was *Medea*. We found it not inspired, though with passages of considerable beauty. But what was dazzlingly beautiful was the sight of the audience. Roman society had turned out in full number to do homage to the Senator, and I have not seen anywhere such magnificent dresses. I do not believe in America such elaborate clothes have been worn since what we now call the fabulous twenties. But certainly their dresses here bore no faintest resemblance to those skimpy models. These made use of yards upon yards of brocade, lace, heavy satin, taffeta of such substance it could stand alone. There was not one little basic black dress among them. These were creations of such originality each could certainly only be worn a very few times.

The porter at the hotel had been a little anxious about selling us tickets and had finally revealed the source of his anxiety by inquiring nervously if we would be able to equip ourselves in "full evening"; otherwise, he'd said, he could not sell us seats downstairs. We had assured him we were able and willing to meet these requirements, and as we came out into the foyer for the first intermission, congratulated one another a little smugly on looking smart, though not gorgeous.

It was at that moment we took note of Margie's accessory. We were on our way through the foyer to the bar for a glass of champagne, walking slowly, and we hoped elegantly, when something swinging at Margie's side caught the eye simultaneously of the other three.

Sophy voiced our mutual wonder. "What in the name of God is that?" she asked and pointed.

Margie held up the object in one hand, not in itself an easy thing to do. It was the largest knapsack handbag I think I have ever seen, and it was of bright mustard-colored leather. With this, Margie was wearing a dress of black lace and chiffon in clinging lines, large and very beautiful diamond pendant earrings, matched with a dazzling breastplate. We queried Margie about her choice of evening bag.

Margie's eyes are as blue and candid as a child's. She looked from one to the other of us. "Why," she said, "I didn't think anyone would notice it." She strode ahead of us toward the bar, swinging vigorously by the handle the mustard beauty.

We huddled close together as we sipped our champagne at the bar, partly in order to hide Margie's bag and also because by comparison with the creatures swaying past us, we suddenly felt we had been dressed by the village dressmaker's apprentice.

We talked about this after the opera on the way home. We weren't resentful of the spectacular dresses we had seen, but we were bewildered by the memory of the frequent appeals each of us receives at home to help a starving Italian child. Zella said it wasn't because our own country was such a Utopia of luxury for everyone, but the contrast at home wasn't so startling, and besides we hadn't needed help to restore war-demolished cities.

I broke in. "I've tremendous admiration," I said, "for the amount of rebuilding that's going on." I explained to Margie: "We couldn't miss seeing it from the train windows in every town we passed, and Milan is as busy as a swarm of bees. It all shows vitality, a refusal to stay down. I haven't said this aloud before," I went on, "because I love Paris and the French so much, but I was sick at heart there at the apathy of people, and in a drive all over Paris, I saw only one bit of scaffolding to indicate even any repair work being done."

Sophy agreed with my sadness about Paris, and added thoughtfully that perhaps the clothes we had seen in Rome that night were good morale builders, and that when you had to push hard, it was necessary to exaggerate somewhere.

We had found Italy and the Italians we had encountered so generous in spirit and warm of heart toward us, we agreed it was churlish to criticize any aspect. Concurring in this, we went to bed.

We were lazy the next morning deliberately. At breakfast I announced to Zella my intention to loll. Zella said she'd like nothing better than to join me in the lack of activity. I was delighted. "If we don't slow up the pace we've set," I protested, "we'll get to be like two women I saw years ago in the Louvre. I heard one of them say to the other, 'Minnie, if you read while I look, we'll get through this in half the time.' "

We were still in our dressing gowns when Margie and Sophy knocked at the door. They were coated, hatted and handbagged for whatever excursion might be suggested. Told of our intention to stay exactly where and as we were, they promptly went back to their own room, and got into their wrappers.

We lunched at the Austrian Embassy with the Princess von Schwarzenburg. There were no other guests. Pussy was as I had remembered her: tall, slender, black-haired and beautiful; all this with a gay humor and a delightful mind, too. At lunch the talk got around to languages and I voiced my dismay at the ineptness of Americans with a foreign tongue. This had followed Zella's comment on the near perfection of our hostess' English, even to idiom.

Margie, who is always interested in every aspect of life between the sexes, asked what language the Prince and Princess spoke when they were alone.

"English," Pussy said. "I think that's because when my husband was courting me, he didn't speak French and I didn't know German. English was the only one we both knew. But," she added, "when we're displeased with each other we speak French. It's more formal."

Before we left, plans were set for a Roman excursion with Pussy as guide. We were starting the next morning, we told her, on a week's motor trip to Florence and the hill towns. When we got

back, she said, she would like to take us on an expedition to places
not emphasized in the guidebooks. We were delighted with this
suggestion. Sophy asked if there were particular things that interested her.

"Well," Pussy said, "when we first came to Rome I realized
there was so much to see one could easily be overwhelmed and,
simply from not knowing what other way to turn, follow the same
tourist path over and over again. You see," she amplified, "I knew
I would be asked many times to take people about the city, visitors
from my husband's country and from my own, Belgium. So I made
a plan that every year I would concentrate on either one period or
one art form." She smiled mischievously, "I'm afraid as a result of
that, visitors in my care have gone home with a very one-sided
impression of Rome."

I asked what side she intended to show us. "I'm prepared to be
more generous with you," she answered. "I'll give you a choice, but
in case you should by any chance be interested in my field of the
moment, it's mosaics."

We settled happily for mosaics on our return.

Zella dined that night at the Hassler with friends of hers she had
encountered in the lobby of the Eden. Sophy, Margie and I stayed
at our own hotel.

Zella had spent the afternoon shopping with another friend from
the American Embassy. Sophy and Margie had coaxed me into a
long and uninteresting walk. As a result we were all tired and I, in
addition, was somewhat put out at the sisters and their passion for
seeking fresh air as a delectable objective in itself. I do not find
this so.

At dinner I pointed out to Sophy and Margie, perhaps with some
asperity, that all Philadelphians I know have one trait in common,
and that is a compelling urge to secure fresh air as if it were a tan-
gible thing, like an edelweiss, that one can clutch in the hand after
a tremendous effort to reach it. I reminded them of the time a
member of their family had come over to New York to meet a boat

arriving from Europe. At six o'clock in the evening, learning that
the boat would not dock until the following morning, he had taken
train back to Philadelphia and a car from there to his house in the
country, in order to capture some fresh air before leaving at six
the following morning, returning to New York.

Our procedure, I said, had followed that pattern. The heels of
our shoes were on a slant from trudging up and down the hills and
streets of Rome as we went sight-seeing. But since we had not
deliberately gone for fresh air, we must make that a special expedition, and so I had been made to stump up and down that afternoon
the paths of the Borghese Gardens, and I had found the place very
dull. They had not cared. They were out for fresh air.

Sophy answered all this with some nonsense about my being the
better for the air. Margie changed the subject, and we concluded
the meal amicably in our accustomed congeniality. But as we came
out of the dining room, I heard my two companions suggest, at the
very same moment, a brisk walk—and this really was scarcely to be
believed—in order to get a little fresh air before going to bed.
I went to bed.

They went for a walk.

Chapter 10

AT NINE-FIFTEEN the following morning the four of us were on the steps of St. Peter's, each with a ticket in hand admitting us to an audience with the Pope. We moved slowly toward the entrance because we were in a tremendous crowd, though the ceremony would not take place until ten o'clock. Ours was not to be a private audience. We were in the company of several thousand people, but we had been told that an audience in St. Peter's would be a memorable sight. Because of the press of people surging in, the four of us were unable to stay together, but Zella and I convened by accident at the base of one of the great marble columns to the right of the center aisle, and about halfway up the nave. We stayed together and from there watched with fascination the kinds of people that were filling the church.

There were delegations, the leader carrying a banner designating the identity of the group. There was every age, from babies carried, to very old people—some of these, too, were carried in. There were family groups; many of these were peasants, their poverty showing through their threadbare clothes and shoes. Some were stylish, their prosperity evident in the beautiful black lace mantillas the women wore. And there was the over-all sound that always comes from a crowd, like surf roaring in on a beach some distance away.

Suddenly, with no announcement, with no fanfare of trumpets, there was His Holiness. He came through a door from the side on which Zella and I were waiting. It was an entrance near the one through which we all had come. He was seated on a chair, the chair in turn placed on a litter borne by members of his special guard. They were in scarlet uniform.

Every member of that dense crowd seemed simultaneously to sense the appearance of the Pope. We all turned in his direction, and that turning made a sound like a sudden wind at night that rushes through trees and is gone, and there was over the church the silence that comes when the wind has passed. But the silence in the church was the length only of a breath; the breath was let out into such a shout of welcome as I had never thought to hear in a church and have seldom heard anywhere. No one had told me it would be like this. I had thought heralds with trumpets would announce the coming of His Holiness, and that when he appeared, everyone would drop to his knees and remain in that position and in reverent silence until the austere figure, with hand upraised in papal blessing, would reach the altar. This was nothing of the sort.

"*Vive Papa, vive Papa,*" the great crowd roared. And on the litter was a man of such finely drawn beauty of face and frailty of body, that had he held the position in which I had imagined I would see him, he would have seemed to be of no earthly substance. But his was no esthetic removal from the world and his people in it, that I had anticipated. With the most beautiful single gesture I think I have ever seen, he circled with one hand then the other, the crowd on either side of him, bringing us to him and with him to the altar. He did this constantly all the way up the aisle. And as he gathered us in with him he smiled in such joyous welcome that I, who am not a Catholic, responded with an uplifting of spirit that brought me a feeling of instant and deep communion with everyone under St. Peter's dome.

I turned involuntarily from the sight a moment, as one does when the sun is suddenly too bright, and saw an old woman standing beside me, so little she came just above my shoulder. She wore shabby black with a woolen shawl over her head. She held her hands, palms pressed together, in front of her. They were coarse-grained, deeply seamed, the knuckles of her fingers swollen and twisted. They were working hands, hard-working hands. I looked from them to her face. Her head was thrown back, she was smiling, but her eyes were closed. I thought she was in happy prayer and knew instantly this was not so. Her eyes were closed because she wasn't tall enough to see over the people in front of her, and so, in resignation, she was acknowledging her nearness to His Holiness.

I tapped her on the arm, she opened her eyes, startled. I pantomimed my conjecture that she couldn't see over the crowd, and she nodded with an acceptance of lack of privilege that I found intolerable. I looked around for Zella. I had forgotten her. She was behind me. She had found room to stand on a narrow ledge part way up a marble column. She had evidently seen my brief exchange with the old woman.

Before I could speak she said, "We can get her up here," and jumped down from her place.

Together we indicated what we wanted to do. The old woman turned from one to the other of us, bewildered, but with a heartbreaking look of trust.

Zella and I said, "One, two, three," across her, and from either side we lifted her, setting her on the little ledge. I took her rough, grizzly hand in mine, holding it to give her balance. I felt it suddenly vibrate like a needle on a compass. I leaned back to look up at her. She had caught sight of His Holiness. Her mouth was half open, her eyes wide and the tears gushed from them down the furrows in her old, worn face.

When His Holiness had left the litter, and from his chair at the High Altar begun to speak, Zella and I lifted her down at her indicated request. She leaned against the column and closed her eyes, listening, and not weeping any more. She clasped her hands again in front of her. The tears dried on her cheeks. I think she didn't know they were there.

It was difficult to hear from where we were standing and I moved away, thinking I couldn't understand, even if I could hear, and so I would look about at the people. But within a few yards I found I was in the direct range of a loudspeaker and to my astonishment discovered the Pope was just concluding a message in beautiful English. I stayed there and heard him speak in French, German, Spanish and Portuguese, and realized he was addressing a delegation from each country in its own language. At the conclusion of these speeches there was a long wait. I think perhaps he was holding private audience with a few small groups of people I had seen conducted to the front before the appearance of His Holiness. They had seemed to be family groups, dressed more formally than the others in the big audience; little girls in white with veils, the boys in Eton suits, women in long black dresses, black mantilla over the head, and the men in evening clothes.

I do not know that special audiences with these people were the cause of the wait. I couldn't see. But it was half an hour before I did see His Holiness, and he was then transferring to the chair on the litter. He came down the aisle just as he had gone up it, smiling and encircling us with one hand and then the other. But this time at intervals, he signaled in some fashion to his bearers to stop. At each of these stops someone near him in the crowd would hold up a small white cap, a duplicate of the one His Holiness was wearing. His Holiness, removing his own, would place on his head for a minute the one proffered him, then return it. Each time he did this the shouting that was constant would swell into a roar, and His Holiness would nod his head in evident pleasure, smiling with such joyousness it was almost audible laughter.

At the end of the center aisle, the bearers stopped once more. The Pope rose to his feet standing on the litter. I cannot believe that was an easy thing to do, and I realized how small of stature he is and how fragile. He might have been made of delicate porcelain. He seemed, against the light from the open doors behind him, almost transparent. Standing, he gave his blessing, sat again on his chair. The bearers turned a corner into the side aisle, the velvet curtains at its end were drawn aside, the litter passed between them, the curtains were dropped. The audience was over.

I found my friends a little ahead of me in a frightening mob that pushed so vigorously toward the doors I was almost lifted off my feet. I was a little panicky, and at that instant, recognizing Sophy in front of me, called out to her.

She heard me and was able only to turn her head in my direction. "Look out for the door," she called back, "keep toward the middle."

Reaching the doorway a minute later I was glad of her warning. I heard a woman cry out and saw she was caught rounding the edge of the door in order to go through, and that her side was pressed into its sharp ridge. No one in her vicinity seemed to pay the slightest attention to her distress and I could not get near her. A sudden surge from behind lifted me off my feet and carried me in a rush through the open doorway. Luckily for me the press around me was so great I was held upright. An Italian crowd is a formidable battering ram. I don't know what happened to the woman.

I joined my friends who were waiting for me on the piazza. Our clothes were twisted, our hats awry. Straightening these we congratulated one another we had got out no more scathed than that, and hailed a taxi.

On the way to the hotel we talked very little beyond saying almost to ourselves that what we had just seen was a ceremony completely different from anything we had anticipated, and one never to be forgotten. But when Margie displayed a package of rosaries she had bought for friends and had taken to be blessed, Zella asked how the package had got so badly torn. Margie answered she had torn it herself, wanting to give the blessing every opportunity to get through.

We reassembled in the hotel lobby after final preparations for our departure on the motor trip. Our large bags had been put in a storeroom to await our return in a week. Margie, following her daily custom, had changed from, and immediately after, back into her blue gabardine suit.

The car, ordered months ahead through a travel agency, was to be at the door at eleven-thirty. We walked up and down in the sunlight outside and sat down in the lobby. At a little after twelve a gentleman appeared and asked for Mrs. Jacobs, in whose name the car had been ordered. Finding her, he reported he needed her signature to secure the proper papers of transfer. To Sophy's inquiry as to why he had not secured this some days before, knowing the time of our arrival in Rome, his response was he had not wanted to disturb her. She signed the paper. He left, promising to return on the instant.

We ordered a Cinzano.

An hour and a half later he returned. We were still in the lobby. Triumphantly he announced the car was waiting even at that moment at the door. We trooped out to find at the curb a dismal, dusty, dirty Fiat. Leaning dejectedly against it was a man of a seedy appearance that coincided exactly with that of the car. Our harbinger of this vehicle introduced him as a partner.

Sophy is one who is always on the side of peace. She will make almost any concession to avoid an argument. Of the group I am counted the one most aggressive, ready for belligerence. But it was Sophy who stepped forward from where the four of us stood silent.

Sophy faced the two men. "You are renting us this car in this condition?" she demanded.

"Si, si, si, Signora," they both answered. "Fine car," one of them said. "No trouble," the other volunteered.

Sophy rounded on that speaker. "There's going to be trouble," she said, "right now. I ordered a car three months ago. Wasn't that time enough to get it washed?"

It was a rhetorical question and Sophy put up her hand, palm toward them, refusing to be answered. She went to the car, opened the door and looked in. We came close and over her shoulder saw an ash tray overflowing with cigarette stubs, the carpet muddy and the seats far from clean. Her head in the interior, Sophy let flow back an expression of her displeasure that was beautiful to hear but it surprised the three of us.

We had not known, we said, when later we were paying tribute to Sophy, she possessed such a fruity vocabulary. Sophy admitted she hadn't known she knew these words either. They had just seemed to come to her.

Even if the man did not understand their literal meaning, he could not have mistaken their general sense. Listening, as I stood in the sunlight on the sidewalk, I found it hard to realize that less than two hours before we had all been awed into silence by a religious experience with the Pope.

Sophy withdrew, straightened up and turned to face us. "Well," she said and her voice was restored to its usual gentle tone, "well," she said, "what do you want to do? Shall we demand a new car or risk this one?"

But we simultaneously and without vote had recognized a leader by her force of oratory. We paid the homage that was due it and her.

Zella was our spokesman. "Whatever you say," she said respectfully.

Sophy walked ruminatively around the car and kicked each tire hard as she passed it. Both men flinched, but said nothing. Sophy said something. "The tires," she told them, "have practically no tread at all, as you very well know."

One of the men started to speak, but again she forbade conversation with the gesture of a police officer halting traffic. She addressed herself to us in a lower tone, moving us a little distance away from the two cowed men who were leaning more toward than against the trunk of a tree at the curb, as if they wished they could climb it and hide in its upper branches.

"As a matter of fact," Sophy said confidentially, "I think the car is really all right, except that it's so filthy. And that makes me so mad I'd like to throw it in the teeth of that travel agency. But on the other hand if we demand a new one, at the rate of time it's taken us to get this one from these dolts, we'll be here two or three days more probably. And we'll be all crossed up in our itinerary and the hotel reservations we've made. What do you think?"

We made it plain the decision must be hers.

"Captain," I said, "whatever you say goes."

She went back to the men. "Empty that ash tray," she ordered. "Brush out the inside and we'll take the car."

I don't know how much they understood, but they got the idea and fell over each other in their eagerness to get us on our way and out of their sight. I don't know either how they cleaned the inside of the car; with their hands probably, but they cleaned it. We were busy supervising the stowing of the luggage in the back. When we prepared to embark, the car looked considerably better than it had looked a few minutes before. Both men bowed us in as if they were footmen handing us into a Royal Daimler, instead of two disreputable scoundrels getting rid of us in a very poor Fiat.

Sophy took the wheel, of course. "All right, everybody?"

We answered with a chorus of "Okay."

"We're off!" she said.

The group of porters that had brought our luggage paused on the sidewalk to wave, the manager of the hotel was there to wish us *bon voyage*, Zella's two friends who were stopping at the Eden happened to come out of the hotel and they waved.

Sophy put her foot on the starter. The man who had delivered the car stuck his head through the window. "Pardon, Signora," he said gently, "alas, no petrol." He smiled reassuringly. "My friend and I push." He pointed ahead of him.

The Eden Hotel stands on the crest of a slight hill. At its bottom we saw a gas station.

None of us could think of anything to say. Scoundrel one withdrew from the window and hurried past us toward the rear of the car. Scoundrel two evidently joined him.

Sophy gripped the wheel, breathing hard. We felt a slight preliminary motion and then we began to roll slowly. Our band of
well-wishers in front of the hotel called cries of *"Bon voyage,"*
"Arrivederci," "Have a good time."

We gathered a little speed, and as we curled over the brim and
started the descent down the hill Sophy spoke.

She said only one word, but she said it loud and clear, and it was
a beauty.

Chapter 11

AT HALF-PAST two that afternoon we were climbing a steep and winding hill into a little town called Narni. To Sophy's discomfiture, but our relief, we were rolling up it as easily as we had taken the down grade under manpower at our departure. The dirty little Fiat had merited 100 for deportment; no coughing, sputtering, lagging, no recalcitrance of any sort.

I had not been so even tempered as "little Fiat." I had voiced, in shrill staccato at every turn, my nervous disapproval of Italian motorists. The greater number of them we had discovered travel on motorcycles or bicycles with some sort of engine attached. But they *all* travel as if jet-propelled, and they all employ a singular and hair-raising code of signals. Instead of anticipating with the horn a curve that someone else might be approaching from the other side, they round the curve first, and then blow loud in full view of and practically no distance from us. The only travelers who move with sanity are drivers of carts drawn by bullocks.

I had voiced another grievance, though not with such repetition as my yelp at each charge on us from around a curve by a motorist. I had said more than once, however, that I did not understand how the Italian, tending ordinarily to overstatement, could name "hill towns" the mountain fastnesses we had already reached. And I had predicted gloomily that things were going to get steeper. I had called on my friends to admit their knowledge of my horror of heights and winding narrow roads up mountains. And I had begged them to tell me honestly if they could call a hill any of the summits we had topped.

Sophy and Zella in the front seat had paid my laments no mind. Zella, the only one besides Sophy who could read a map, had been appointed map-reader, and was engrossed in joyous reiteration to Sophy that we were on the map exactly where we were actually on the road. This has always seemed to me the silliest kind of corroboration, but it is one in which map-readers take particular and perpetual delight. Margie, however, in the back seat with me, had been soothing, urging me to view the landscape and not the road ahead.

At such times as I had been able to move my head from side to side, instead of rigidly face front, I had been soothed and even uplifted in spirit by field after field of bright colored flowers, not any of which I recognized, except the scarlet poppies, and they outnumbered all the rest. There were bullocks in the fields, so gleaming white they might have been scrubbed with a kitchen cleanser, and working with them were men and women with vivid yellow, red, green, blue bandannas tied around their heads; a happy sight to see on a sunny day.

But at half-past two at the top of a hill into the little village of Narni, we were hungry.

Even Captain Jacobs and the map-reader accepted without protest Margie's and my suggestion we stop for food. I am conceded by my traveling companions to have one usefulness on a trip. They do not count it on a par with their areas of competence but they do grant it comes in handy. Years of traveling about my own country on lecture tours have developed in me a talent like a dowser's. I can find a good hotel and a good restaurant.

I left my friends in a modern souvenir shop that also carried refreshments, and set off along the cobbled street in the direction from which we had come. I'd thought as we passed a low building, that it had the look of an inn though there was no sign outside. I found the place again, pushed open the door and went in.

A few minutes later I had rescued the other three from an imminent purchase of gruesome-looking provisions, and was ushering them through the door I had recently opened. "I didn't take time," I told them, "to find out if there's anyone here who can give us some lunch. I was so afraid you were going to buy some gunk, and," I added, "I was so right. But I have a feeling this is a good place."

I went ahead of them through a room with a bare scoured floor, one or two chairs and nothing else in it. At the far side I opened another door and was in a kitchen. Two girls and an older woman were at a table there, eating. They looked up startled at my appearance on the threshold. One of the young girls got up and came toward me.

I told her there were four of us and asked if we might have some lunch.

She looked doubtful and made me understand this was an inn, the Albergo Bella Vista, but there were no guests at the moment. People came in the summer. She was truly distressed that they had no food to give. I knew she thought we expected an elaborate meal.

I asked if by any chance they had some bread and some butter, perhaps, and maybe cheese.

She beamed with relief and pleasure. The two women at the table behind her laughed aloud. But of course they had that, she told me.

"And a bottle of wine?" I asked.

She nodded once more, and went ahead of me through the door I had just entered, indicating I was to follow.

I gathered up the three others in the outer room and went with them into an adjoining one on the far side of the kitchen. The room was dark, but the girl going through the doorway ahead of us raised a window shade and we saw we were in a small dining room with perhaps five or six tables in it. We sat at the table by the window with the raised shade, and looked down a sheer drop to valleys below and mountains beyond. When the girl had left us we ventured to open the window. The air was a little chilly but delicious, and the sun bright. Sophy raised the shades at the other windows. We walked down the line of them looking out at the magnificent view. Margie went back to the car for her mink stole.

I can still remember that lunch, and I shall never taste anything much better. We had come at the very moment when fresh baked bread was taken from the oven. We ate it hot, the crust crackling between our teeth, the butter melting as we spread it. They made the cheese, too, the girl told us, and the wine was from their own locality.

When we finally left, the meal had cost less than a dollar for the four of us. I was in favor again with my friends, and the trip ahead of us was again in favor with me.

The Brufani Hotel in Perugia is on the crest of a hill higher than the one supporting the Albergo Bella Vista in Narni. And I had classified the Narni hill a mountain.

We came to Perugia about eight o'clock that night. It was very light, the streets were crowded but we took no time to explore them because once more we were hungry. We had drinks in the bar and ate in the hotel dining room; very good food, beginning as always with a minestrone. We were given a table adjoining one occupied by a very stout lady dining alone. She provided a divertissement we found absorbingly interesting but mechanically puzzling. At the end of each course the zipper on the side of her dress, and happily for us the side we could see, slowly descended the full length of its cable, opening behind as it traveled a wide expanse of bright pink girdle. Just before knifing into the ensuing course, our neighbor would close up the gap, returning the zipper to its starting point, and there it would stay until, coincident with her last mouthful, it slid down the trolly again. Since her meal totaled six courses —soup, fish, entree, salad, dessert, cheese and fruit—we were given opportunity to verify the accurate timing of this phenomenon. Our own conversation in consequence of this preoccupation was spasmodic and desultory.

Our rooms looked down on the street in front of the hotel. Leaning out a little over the window sill we could see, to the right, a little green park along a palisade, that on the other side of a protecting iron railing dropped away to the valley far below.

Zella and I had stood at our windows briefly before going down to dinner and had seen the palisade crowded with people strolling along it. But when we returned to our rooms and looked out again about half-past nine, the whole promenade and square beneath our windows were deserted. We surmised that evidently there is a specific hour when one strolls along the palisade and when that hour is ended, the Perugian goes home. We went to bed.

Next morning at breakfast Zella told us about a festival she had come upon in her guidebook reading in bed the night before. She had not dared wake me at the time, she told us, lest my response be unsympathetic. Breakfast, she hoped, would warm us to her proposal. The paragraph she read reported a festival called "The Feast of the Candles" and occurring once a year on May 15 in the town of Gubbio.

"Today," she reminded us, "is the fifteenth of May, and Gubbio is not far from Assisi. We're going to Assisi anyway. What do you say to Gubbio?"

We said "yes" unanimously and enthusiastically. We asked the porter, that master mind of every European hotel, at what time the Candle Ceremony at Gubbio would take place. To get the information we requested necessitated a good deal of thumb-wetting on his part and turning many pages forward and then back again in a guidebook that from its raddled look might have been published before the outbreak of the First World War. But eventually he wrested from it the information that the Candle Ceremony took place around six o'clock in the afternoon.

This was good news; we would be able to explore Perugia, visit

Assisi, and go to Gubbio. We set out on the instant to see Perugia
by two separate methods. Sophy and Margie took the guidebook
way, Zella and I strolled, and I think we had the better time.

We found tents and booths of a market covering the whole of
a wide thoroughfare, except for one center aisle left free for vehicles. If there is any commodity that was not for sale there, I
cannot name it. I saw clothes, shoes, hats for men, women and
children. I bought a pair of white buckskin low-heeled slippers
from the man who had made them. His wife helped me try them
on. I stood in the street, one hand resting on her shoulder as she
bent down to remove the shoe I was wearing and slip underneath
my foot a piece of cardboard, so that I should not have to step
on the street. The shoemaker supervised the fitting, took the slippers from me, worked on them a minute or two, returned them.
His wife stooped down, I put my hand on her shoulder, tried them
on again and found them a perfect fit. They cost seventy-nine
cents.

A little farther on I bought, for presents, eight shopping bags
made of strips of white tape about half an inch wide woven and
knotted like raffia, and with drawstrings long enough to hang over
the shoulder. I found very smart sweaters for my daughters, a suit
for my small grandson, and also for him a charming hat made of
candy-stripe cotton in pink and white, shaped like a jockey hat,
an adjustable strap under the chin. This headgear, its maker
assured me, was safe protection from the dangerous sun.

Zella was making purchases at the same time. We both attracted
a small group of interested and charming advisers.

Our return to the hotel was slow and unsteady. We had to feel
our way along the the cobblestones; because of the number and
size of the purchases we carried, our area of vision was restricted.
I had spent for all these just under ten dollars. Zella, I'm sure,
had not put out more than that. We left our loot in our room
and returned to the street for sightseeing.

We found Sophy and Margie at the Fonte Maggiore, the great

fountain. They joined us to see again the Church of San Pietro and led us to the Oratory of San Bernardine. I can pay no higher tribute when I say I would motor again up the hills to Perugia to see them.

At half-past eleven we were ready to go on to Assisi, though packing the car took a little more time and considerable more maneuvering and shifting than had been necessary the day before. Zella and I did not need to have Sophy point out to us that the reason for this was our morning's activities. But Sophy did point this out.

We were in Assisi in time for lunch and there I made a grievous mistake.

The drive had been beautiful. We hadn't hurried, we had pointed out to one another constantly, to have the added pleasure of sharing the sight of flowers, meadows, bullocks, people, views. But the road into Assisi is like a top turned upside down. The area included in each turn grows smaller and smaller until I thought it impossible for the car to go any higher, at least with me in it. At the point where I made this declaration, and it was more a point than a curve, I saw a sign reading "Hotel Windsor." I implored Sophy to stop the car and allow us to lunch there, suggesting also that those who wanted, after lunch, could go to the summit, on foot or by car. This would allow freedom of choice. My friends were generously tolerant of my squeamishness and Sophy parked the car.

We lunched at the Windsor on bread, cheese and wine; a scantier meal, the waiter made apparent, than they liked to serve. The hotel itself is comfortable, the view from it magnificent, and it is only just below the square from the great Church of St. Francis. But unhappily for me, my three friends after lunch went the rest of the way to the summit in the car and found there a restaurant. Apart from giving me this information on their return, there had been very little conversation on the subject. But Zella's diary for that day reads: "Lunched at Hotel Windsor because

Emily was afraid to go farther." And Sophy's says briefly, "Windsor Hotel. This was a mistake. We should have gone up to the top of the mountain to the Café D'Italia."

While the three of them were making this discovery, I was wandering happily along the narrow streets below, nosing about in a shop here and there, and emerging from one of these with a charming hand-made blouse.

We were four again at St. Francis' Church, however, and as one in our love of it. Some of the Giottos were shockingly damaged by dampness, but the one of St. Francis and the Birds is exquisite. Standing in front of a Cimabue I thought, "This is like being in a place you think you've seen before in a dream. How long have I known about St. Francis of Assisi? One of the first stories my mother ever told me, and I think she was the first to tell me too, was about Giotto and Cimabue, showing me reproductions of their pictures. And for a long time after that I didn't know Assisi was a place, I thought it was part of St. Francis' name. And then there was the classroom in Miss Faulkner's School in Chicago where we took history of art and passed about from one to another postcard reprints of Giottos and Ciambues. After that, a history of art class at college. There we saw these same reproductions on a screen. And look where I'm standing now! Seeing Cimabues and Giottos."

We joined, one by one, a group that was being conducted by a French monk. He was so endearing in his joy of the place and his eagerness to share its beauty, it would have been churlish to stay aloof. Margie, I thought however, was overdoing her response to his charm when she took the entire tour twice, and was starting on the third round when Sophy nabbed her and restored her to our group. This was not to Margie's pleasure.

At half-past three we were on our way to Gubbio, driving through the Umbrian countryside that had spread so wide below us from the church. It was naïve of us, I suppose, to exclaim at the similarity between the landscape around us and the landscape the

Umbrian painters put on canvas. Nevertheless, we did exclaim about it, and each admitted a previous supposition that the curiously precise fields and little trees had been the painter's own stylizing of what he saw, basing the supposition on the fact that none of us had actually seen such a countryside. But here it was, and the little trees were the supports of grapevines that hung like festoons in rows between them.

Somewhere a clock struck five as we started to climb the steep road that leads into the town of Gubbio.

Chapter 12

FROM FIVE O'CLOCK to half-past six on the afternoon of
Friday, May 15, Margie, Sophy, Zella and I were bystanders
at one of the most extraordinary spectacles any of us had ever
witnessed, the more extraordinary, perhaps, because not one of us
had the faintest idea of what was going on, nor could we find out.
Now I have learned something about it, but I should like to tell
first what we saw.

Sophy drove the car up and up a narrow cobbled street, the
only way into town, it seemed to us. On either side tall dark
houses were so close together there was no space between, and
they came to the very edge of the street itself. Now and then
we passed a branch road going back in the direction from which
we had come, but at so sharp an angle the car could not have
made the turn had we wanted to go that way, and so we kept
on climbing.

We came, without a warning of any previous spacing between
houses, to a turnout that was like an alcove in the road, because
the houses still followed its outline fringing it solidly. But there
was space in the alcove for cars. Sophy drove into this but we
hesitated to leave the car there lest it be forbidden. As we were
debating a man came up to us from behind the car. He was
dressed in a frock coat and wore a large three-cornered hat with

a tall silver buckle on it. A heavy chain of silver links hung around
his neck, and suspended from this was a medallion not much
smaller than a butter plate. Sophy asked if we might leave the car.
He gave us permission and indicated in pantomime we must
proceed on foot.

We got out of the car. Margie debated the advisability of taking
her mink stole in case it should grow chilly, against the safety of
leaving it in the car. Sophy assured her impatiently she would
lock the car and Margie could hide the stole on the floor. Margie
decided to take the stole. Sophy locked the car and we started on
foot. Margie decided she would be more comfortable without the
stole. They returned to the car. Sophy unlocked it, Margie put her
stole on the floor.

Zella and I were waiting for them in the street itself. I happened
to glance a little to my right, up a fork leading down into our
street like the ones we had passed on our way up, and I called
out sharply to Margie and Sophy to come quickly. Zella was staring with me. Advancing toward us down the fork was a religious
procession. At its head was a group of young priests carrying three
effigies, life-size, of saints perhaps, but in the robes and miters of
a bishop. These were in cloth of gold. Immediately behind them
came three officials of the church walking abreast and dressed in
precisely the robes worn by the figures that were carried. These
three walked alone, and behind them a procession divided into
two lines; one made up of little choirboys in scarlet robes with
white tunics, the other, of young men in purple robes and white
tunics.

At the juncture of the fork with the road we were on, the procession turned sharply right and passed us, ascending in the direction the gentleman with the silver chain had indicated for us to
take.

We started after the procession, but we were delayed by Margie's
decision to retrieve her stole. Zella and I returned with her and

Sophy to the car. When we got back to the road intersection, the procession was out of sight, but we set after it hurriedly.

Some quarter of a mile farther up, our street ended in a very large square. A good many people were walking about there, but the procession had vanished. I do not know to this day what became of it. We never saw it again.

At the far side of the square was a cathedral. We walked toward that. A flight of steps ran the entire width of its façade. We climbed these steps and looked around us. On our right a high railing marked the boundary of the square. Beyond it a sheer, deep drop ended far below in what was evidently the town proper. We could see a little park, shops and a great crowd of people. We were aware for the first time of gay music, and saw that it came from a carousel, and that some sort of fair was in full fête below. Directly in front of us, on the opposite side of the square, was a large building that looked as if it might be a town hall. Between that and the church where we stood, along our left side was a row of very handsome houses, several stories high and with balconies running along the front on each floor. There were people sitting on these balconies and others standing or sitting in the open French windows behind them.

The reason we had not distinguished at first the music of the carousel, was that overhead, from the tower of the church, the bell was ringing in broken rhythm, like someone tapping a Morse code in slow time: one, two; one, two, three; one; one, two, three. By putting our heads far back we could just make out figures of men in the belfry pulling the bell ropes that controlled the bell.

The square was filling up. A number of people joined us on the steps, all of them speaking Italian. Margie made several charming overtures in French, but these were met with pantomimes of polite and regretful ignorance of the language.

Sophy picked out a family group not far from us, pointed it out to me and whispered her certainty its members were, by their appearance, American or Scandinavian. It was a strikingly handsome family: father, mother, two boys and a girl, all of them very blonde and blue-eyed. Sophy walked over to them and came back a minute later. "Italians," she said, "not a word of French or English."

In a brief space of silence between bell strokes from above, I heard the sound of a motor, and saw a truck come into the square and stop at a far corner between the railing and the town hall, or whatever that building was. The truck bore a sign identifying it as a mobile radio unit. Two men got out of the front seat, opened up the back of the truck, and began setting up microphone and other equipment. I volunteered to try French or English on the radio men. "They must get around," I said, "they're sure to speak more than one language."

They spoke only Italian, and gathered from what I said I wanted to talk over the microphone, and were gaily willing to allow me this privilege, counting it a fine joke. I scuttled back to my friends on the steps after declining with considerable embarrassment their generous offer.

The tempo of the bell quickened until it was ringing in sharp insistent beat and mounting strength.

Suddenly, and now it was about ten minutes to six, we saw a mob at the mouth of the street we'd followed. They ran toward us, scattering across the wide square, like pebbles shaken out of a bottle.

The four of us admitted to each other afterward that the sight of this crowd pouring at us had set up a panic. We had thought people would never stop coming and that we might be flattened against the façade of the church, trapped there. As it was, we were, in no time at all, squeezed so tight by the press of people all around us, we could not have turned had we wanted to, let alone get away.

Now the bell was screaming in staccato urgency, like a bell on an ambulance or a fire engine.

Three men on horseback galloped into the square from behind the cathedral. They wore white breeches and yellow tunics with bright red sashes. The bell stopped. All the space about the church was so densely packed I did not know how it was possible for the horsemen to make passage other than over bodies. But they did, reining in their horses directly in front of us. From there they moved forward, and at a trot, into the center of the square. I would have said the crowd could not have given so much as an inch, but it gave, by backing and squeezing, space enough for the three horsemen to cut among the people a path that made a wide circle around the center of the square. Each time they made the circuit they widened the circle until they could ride three abreast. Evidently satisfied with their work, they rode off in the direction from which they had come. The crowd stayed as it was.

Immediately they had left, there was a sound of rushing feet. From the direction the horsemen had taken, came three litters, each as big as a farm cart. They were carried on the shoulders of, I guessed, fifteen men, perhaps more, running with the speed of a man doing a fifty-yard dash in a track meet. Topping each of these litters was a structure in black wood, at least fifteen feet high, shaped something like a chessman, and at the peak of each of these, an effigy like the three we had seen on our arrival carried in the religious procession.

The crowd went mad at the sight of them; yelling, screaming, waving their arms, the men shouting. As the startling procession raced around the path that had been cleared for it, occasionally a young man would leave his place at the litter, and instantly be replaced by another from the sidelines, who anticipating such an opportunity had taken off his coat and opened his shirt. They completed the circle five times, and then still running, were out of sight. The ceremony was over.

The crowd went back the way it had come, but more slowly this time, the people laughing and talking to one another.

We were among the last to leave. We sat on the steps while the crowd thinned, but we had little to say to one another.

I think we were all excited, but dazed by what we had seen, and by our bewilderment at not understanding it.

We found the crowd again. It was in the town below at the fair. We had got this far easily in the car. But when we reached, in the town, the blockade that less than an hour ago had advanced toward us in the square, Sophy said we were really stuck now, and would simply have to sit it out. But a man a few feet away from us, elbowing and shoving his way along, called out and pantomimed that we should keep going and blow the horn. Sophy did this; kept going a foot at a time and blew the horn. And people gave way as they had given way to the horsemen; not nervously, not with any sense of alarm, but turning back and laughing at us, at the sound of our horn, and at a gentle impact from our fender.

The way from Gubbio to Perugia is not through the hills, it is over mountains. Zella writes in her diary, "We felt we were driving along the rim of the earth." My own feeling was that at any moment we might leave the earth, either over the rim or at the agency of a motorist coming, as they did come by the score, around the curve at sixty or more, on the wrong side of the road, that was our side, and with the signal on the horn only after we had seen each other.

However, as we drove a new moon climbed the sky and the countryside was strange and beautiful under its soft light.

In the square at Perugia, we were blocked by another crowd. We detoured around this one. It was a Communist meeting. And only two hours away from the medieval ceremony we had witnessed! It was gratifying to observe that ours had drawn the bigger audience.

At the Hotel Brufani we asked manager, clerk, porter, everyone, the meaning of the ceremony we had seen in Gubbio. No one knew. We asked in Florence and in Rome. We asked everyone we knew, and everyone we met. No one could tell us.

Home again in America, I was told about a little book on

Gubbio that has a considerable title: *L'Italia Monumentale* and under that *Collezione Di Monografie, Sotto II Patronato Del Touring Club Italiano*. It is written in Italian and in succeeding chapters first a French and then an English translation is given.

This is what it says about Gubbio:

The origin of Gubbio is lost in antiquity. This is attested by its Pre-Roman walls, by cinerary urns and coins belonging to the Umbro-Roman period and by the celebrated bronze Tables preserved in the Civic Museum. . . . In the eleventh century Gubbio became a free commune and entered on the most glorious period of her history. Her power increased with the growth of her population which included many distinguished men; many of her finest buildings were erected and she long enjoyed her liberty and independence which she knew how to maintain, notwithstanding internal discord and plots woven against her by external enemies. . . . So great were the strength and vitality of the free commune of Gubbio that its powerful neighbour, Perugia, was never able to subdue it, even for a day, though Perugia herself rose to be, after Florence and Siena, the principal centre of Guelph domination in central Italy. . . . In 1151 eleven neighbouring cities, having formed an alliance against the powerful commune of Gubbio, invaded its territory with a large army and beseiged the city, but the courage of the inhabitants was proof against all danger. They placed themselves under the command of their Bishop, Ubaldo, who, laying down his crozier and taking up the sword, gained such a signal victory over the enemy that it was looked upon as nothing less than a miracle. . . . The characteristic Festa dei Ceri, which is celebrated at Gubbio every year on the 15th of May, (the eve of the festival of St. Ubaldo) is perhaps a survival of public rejoicings instituted in commemoration of this great victory. . . . The ceri that probably represent war-chariots or carrocci taken from the enemy cities, are hollow, polygonal wooden structures, each about fifteen feet high. . . . On the summit of the cero belonging to the stone-masons, is posed the statue of St. Ubaldo; the figure of St. George crowns the cero of merchants and traders, while St. Anthony the Abbot is the patron of the agriculturists. On May 15th, after the relics of St. Ubaldo have been carried in procession through the city, the ceri . . . are blessed by the Bishop of Gubbio and carried triumphantly through the streets. . . . Each cero is fitted into a strong wooden stand called a barella and borne by huge shafts on the shoulders of privileged men

known as ceraioli. . . . Finally toward evening, the ceri are brought
into Piazza della Signora where the bearers drink the wine offered by
the Magistrates of the commune to give them strength for the mad
race up the steep slopes of Monte Ingino to the church of St. Ubaldo,
the permanent resting-place of the ceri until the next festival. It is an
arduous task to scale the hill-side bearing the heavy ceri, in a wild
struggle for precedence, but the hundred stalwart ceraioli know no
fatigue in their ardour for the honour of the corporations they represent. The ceremony which has taken place annually for hundreds of
years, terminates with songs.*

On the way down into the village in the car, Margie, leaning out
the window, had kept insisting she saw something that looked like
those effigies, far up on the mountain. But we had told her that
was impossible. Those heavy litters could not possibly have been
carried to a mountaintop.

Margie had been right.

---

* I recommend a little book about Gubbio that has nothing to do with
the festival. It is called *The Seven Miracles of Gubbio and the Eighth, a
Parable* by Raymond Leopold Bruckberger, Illustrated by Peter Lauck.

Chapter 13

THE NEXT morning, early, I shut myself firmly in my room and waved off my chums on another sight-seeing walk around Perugia. I had a piece to write that must go off airmail to CBS in New York to be read on my radio program by my alter program conductor, Harry Marble. By half-past ten when the others came back I had finished, and we set off in the Fiat on the last lap to Florence.

From Perugia to Arezzo the way is lovely, past Trasimeno and smaller lakes, all of them deep blue; and everywhere, coming up to the very rim of the water, fields of scarlet poppies, and always overhead, swallows flying. If I were to take a word association test, and the word given me were Italy, I would put down immediately, I'm sure, red poppies, white bullocks and swallows.

We stopped in Arezzo briefly. We left the car in an open square in the upper section of the town and set out on foot to find Petrarch's house. We had come up the inevitable steep road that marks the approach to every hill town and had emerged on the inevitable square into which the approach empties. I was complaining a little as we started back down the hill on foot. I had been for days, I said, on a perpetual slant. If we explored many more hill towns I would present a very odd appearance by the time we reached England, something like the Tower of Pisa, walking. Furthermore, I was in a chronic condition of thinness of breath, what with the actual demands made on it when I was on foot, and my inner compulsion when in a car to hold it and at the same time push in order to get the Fiat and us to the summit.

I stopped my lament when I saw a man sunning in front of a little house. I asked him the way to the Petrarch Accademia. I had learned from Mr. Clark's guidebook that Petrarch's house was the headquarters of the Accademia.

Later, in the car as we moved on to Florence, Sophy harked back to this moment of my inquiry, using it as an example of my habitual involvement of the group in unwanted associations. It has been a long-standing contention between us developed through years of motor trips together. My subject for debate is that Sophy will never voluntarily ask directions of anyone, preferring either to wander or to sit in the car drawn up at the side of the road for what seems to me an interminable time, crouched over a map plastered against the steering wheel in front of her, as if she were in meditation before the Delphic Oracle awaiting a guiding sign from it. Simply to ask a passerby evidently humiliates both her and her oracle. I had not reminded her, I said, of this trait since the day we registered at the Berlitz School. Sophy's retort was her invariable counterattack that, if permitted, I would substitute passing travelers for mileposts and refer to them in the same frequency as the position of those landmarks, one to every mile, and that this procedure, since I am by nature loquacious, is not conducive to rapid progress. Furthermore, she is wont to point out, I sometimes take the milepost along with us, not always a particularly agreeable association.

Since the morning of May 16, the gentleman sunning himself in Arezzo has been one of her favorite examples of this sort of association. That gentleman, when I questioned him, leaped to his feet, pointed straight ahead of us in the direction in which we were already set—Sophy reminds me of this—and asked, "You Americans?"

I was the one who answered; the others moved ahead rapidly. "Yes," I said, "we are."

The man joined me at once and was with me when I caught up with my friends.

"I American, too," he told us all.

Sophy groaned and said to her companions, "You see what I mean?"

Their response was to close in with her and gang up against me. I felt it instantly.

The newcomer continued, "I from Chicago. Anybody know Chicago?"

I still think it would have been rude not to answer, though pressure has been brought to bear on me to admit this was where I made my greatest mistake.

"Yes," I said, "I know Chicago. I grew up there."

I thought for a moment the man would throw his arms around me and kiss me. He came perilously close, but stopped, his face pushed into mine, his arms wide. "Why I ever leave Chicago?" he demanded. "Tell me that. Chicago the most wonderful city in the world. You know the Loop?"

"Yes," I said, backing away a little. "I know it."

"You know wonderful store of Marshall Field?"

"Yes," I said, "I do. I worked there once."

With a deep sigh he lowered his arms, took my right hand in both his, causing my guidebook, notebook and sweater I was carrying under that arm, to fall to the ground. "Chicago is most beautiful city in whole world," he declared while we both endeavored to pick up the objects that had fallen, not an easy process since he continued to hold my hand in one of his. "Why am I such fool to leave most beautiful city in world?"

The others, once more, had moved on ahead of me. Sophy called back over her shoulder, "Don't tell him, I beg of you."

I compromised. "Well, why were you?" I asked. He released my hand and with both of his beat his breast.

"Because I think I am homesick for Italy. Because I am a fool. Because I do not know enough to stay where I am making good money, live good, raise my children good. No. What I do? I bring them all to Italy. I talk to them years about Italy. I want them to see where papa grow up, papa's old friends. We come. And what happen? Friends have forgot papa. I have forgot them. Children no like it. Wife no like it. I no like it anymore. So what happens?"

We had caught up with the others standing in front of Petrarch's house. Sophy spoke briefly to me. "It wasn't very difficult to find," she said, and turned to the others. "Do we want to go on with *this*," she asked, "and hear all about Chicago, or should we give up the whole thing and go on to Florence?"

They decided to go to Florence. No one asked me to vote. We turned, and like the King of France, marched right up the hill again.

My companion was momentarily put off in his narrative. "You no want to see this place?"

"My friends think we must be on our way," I explained.

"Okay," he agreed cheerfully, and turned back with me. "Nothing much to see anyway. Very old. Everything in Italy, very old. Too old. Not new like Chicago."

"Well, why don't you go back to Chicago?" I asked, and began as usual to wheeze a little as the grade became steeper.

My wandering minstrel stopped in the road, flinging out his arms again. "Why I not go back?" he repeated dramatically. "You ask me that. Because in this dumb country, I no make enough money to get us all back again."

I had not stopped with him. I was endeavoring to keep up with my friends.

He hurried after me. "Maybe I work for you?" he suggested.

I heard a deep groan from Sophy ahead of us.

"Because you love Chicago," he continued. "I work hard, and one day I bring my family back. We all work for you. See Chicago. See the Loop again."

We had reached the car. The others were already in it and Sophy put her foot on the starter. I jumped in and closed the door quickly after me.

The Chicagoan looked wistfully into the back seat, but I held the door firmly. The window was down and I spoke through it. "No," I said, "I can't take you."

Zella addressed the other three. "Well," she said, "we can be glad of that, anyway."

I had opened my purse, relinquishing for a moment my hold on the door, and from a compartment that held a small fund for emergencies, I drew a dollar bill. I counted this an emergency. "Here is something," I said, "to remind you of America," and handed it to him.

The car began to move away from him. He was holding the dollar bill between his hands and was kissing it. "Don't forget," I called back to him, "you didn't like it when you were there. I think it's lovely here."

He checked a kiss on its way to the bill. "Bah," he said. "Here I spit," and illustrated on the ground. "Here I kiss," and completed the salute to the American dollar.

We drove off. There was no conversation among us as we descended the hill, but when we came out of the town and into the countryside again, Sophy asked courteously, "Well, now that we haven't seen Arezzo, would you like to tell us about the Loop?"

Chapter 14

WE ARRIVED at the Grand Hotel in Florence in time for late lunch there. We had driven from Arezzo without pause and just within the speed limit, since the landscape of that area, after the beautiful countryside we had traveled the days before, was uninteresting. Our original schedule had allowed us only one night in Perugia, but our excursion to Gubbio had necessitated a second night's stay. Accordingly, at the Grand Hotel in Florence we found our rooms had not been held. The clerk was apologetic but explained the place was crowded. He showed us two rooms at the back of the hotel that looked out over rooftops, and contained in addition to bedroom equipment only a washstand; tub and W.C. were across the hall.

Zella and I were delighted with the view and the washstand. The combination made me feel I was back in the surroundings to which previous trips abroad had accustomed me. But Margie was bitterly disappointed. She did not mind, she assured us, the lack of plumbing equipment. What she did mind, deeply, was the lack of view. She had been in Florence once before when she was seventeen, and had looked then out her hotel on the Arno. As we had approached Florence, she said, she had looked forward more and more excitedly to looking out her bedroom window again and seeing the Arno. It would not be the same to look at the river from a sidewalk. If we would help her to achieve a room with a view, she would not ask, she promised, another special privilege during the remainder of the trip.

No grandmother can resist the plea of another for help in recapturing something of her lost youth, and as a means of recapturing it, Zella and I agreed, a washstand and roofstops could not hold their own against a view of the Arno.

On our way in to lunch we spoke again to the clerk at the desk. That is, Margie spoke. It was beautiful, a heartrending plea that she be allowed once more to look out on her beloved river, the Arno, a river she had always dreamed about. The three of us made a Greek chorus, nodding our heads in agreement, shaking them in sorrow at appropriate cues. The clerk was moved. He would have been a man of stone to have withstood Margie's flight of prose and a delivery of it that had something of the quality Duse might have respected.

When she had finished, her audience assured her he would somehow make it possible for her to realize her dream. He extended his hand across the counter, as a pledge of faith and honor, and Margie wrung it fervently.

We had an omelet for lunch, and a bottle of white wine. Sophy was signing the check when a page came to our table and asked that we stop at the desk. There was a message for us.

Margie was the first to reach it. When the rest of us caught up with her she was leaning across its counter looking into the eyes of the clerk on the other side, and they were bowing almost reverently to each other.

We heard him say, "Yes, is like miracle."

Zella broke in briskly. She is not one for circumlocution. "What happened?" she asked. "Bad news from home or have we got the room?"

Margie turned to face us, her face radiant, her eyes shining. "We have rooms," she said, "two rooms on the Arno!"

"That's fine," Zella conceded generously. "We'd better get our things together right away and move."

"Not only on the Arno," Margie continued dreamily, "but with a balcony. Think of it, Zella. We can lean on the railing of the balcony and look at the Arno." She looked back at the clerk. "Thanking you is not enough," she told him. "You've been so understanding. You know how I feel."

Behind me Sophy muttered, "You're darn right, thanking isn't enough."

I knew she was speaking in her official capacity as banker.

The clerk, with an effort, emerged from his emotional trauma, got a key, came from behind the desk and led us to the elevator. A few minutes later he unlocked the door to the suite and stood aside to let us enter. As Margie passed, he extended his arm toward the interior of the suite. "It is there," he said simply, and Margie hurried past him.

The suite included two rooms and a little hallway, one room immediately at its end, the other to the left. Margie kept straight ahead, Sophy following her. Accordingly, Zella and I turned left and entered a very large and elegant bedroom. We approved its size and elegant furnishings, and then simultaneously moved to one of a pair of French windows on the far side. Zella opened the windows and together we stepped onto a balcony.

I leaned over the rail, following Margie's dream pattern, and looked down. On the other side of the road that passed the hotel was the river Arno, a shallow stream, so muddy that its color was a sickly mustard. On its far side a bank of solid rock rose sharply and, because the river was so low, a great deal of this bank was exposed. Across the greater part of the rocky exposure was a picture in red paint, the size of a Broadway billboard, of a hammer and sickle, over the top of this, the words "VOTA PARTITO COMUNISTA ITALIANO."

When Margie and Sophy came in a few minutes later, Zella and I were writing letters. Sophy proposed we all go for a walk.

"Sight-seeing, or fresh air?" I asked.

Sophy said she didn't really care, she only thought it would be nice to go out. Zella said that appealed to her very much. Margie said nothing. She seemed to me to be subdued.

I think it was in Miss Boyce's history of art class in the Faulkner School in Chicago when I was in eighth grade, I learned that the Cathedral of Santa Maria del Fiore was the greatest cathedral in Florence and usually called the Duomo because of its magnificent dome, and that the Campanile built alongside it to hold its bells was done by the painter Giotto and is always referred to as Giotto's Tower. I saw reproductions of them both at that time, and later, in a history of art course at college, I learned these things again. If asked in an examination I could have identified them. But no one, teacher, fellow student or returned traveler, ever told me that the marble in which these two lovely things were built is in shades of delicate pink and pale green, in dainty stripes and cross bars. I knew the patterns, but the colors astonished me so that, standing on a spot where I had waited thirty years to stand in order to see at last the source of reproductions I had so many, many times held in my hand, I felt no rush of tears at this fulfillment, but an up-surge within, of laughter born of sheer incredulous amazement at delicate pink, pale green, white and touches of blue. This is not the only intellectual surprise I have had over the span of my adult years. There have been enough of them and more, to cement my suspicion into a certainty that I am cloudy-witted. Things my contemporaries with an educational background that corresponds to mine have learned almost synonymously with being taught to read and write, have swum into my ken many years after the day I tipped my mortarboard to a college diploma. They are still swimming in, and I must admit I enjoy the surprise they bring; and I was surprised by my own heretical first impression that the Duomo looked to me like something out of a confectioner's window and a triumphant example of his art.

My pleasure in the interior of the Duomo was not so giddy. I reverenced humbly its majestic proportions, its magnificent space.

When we had left the cathedral and crossed the street to the Baptistery I did not confide to my friends how the Duomo had surprised me, nor how relieved I was to find that the great doors of the Baptistery I had always thought were in bronze, were in bronze.

There was no surprise for me, either, at the Ponte Vecchio when we reached it on our homeward walk to the hotel. I sent up a little prayer of thanksgiving, and I did not mean it to be ironic, that the brilliant accuracy developed in men at war had made it possible, while destroying cities and lives, to leave intact the Ponte Vecchio so that I might find it after waiting so long to see it, exactly as I had thought it would be. A passing glance in the windows of its nearest shops convinced me I would be back the following day.

We dined across the street from the Grand at the Excelsior Hotel. We found it stylish in a stuffy pre-1914 way, and the food excellent. After dinner we had crème de menthe in a little bar in the hotel just to one side of the main entrance. The room was charming, and together with an excellent American pianist, made a setting totally unlike the rest of the hotel.

Zella got up at six the following morning. Before leaving home she had been asked by a newspaper editor in Erie, Pennsylvania, where she and her husband had formerly lived, to write a series of pieces about our trip for the local journal. She had concealed this assignment from us lest, she said in her moment of confession, we heckle her. Goaded by my sleepy but persistent questioning as to what on earth she was doing getting dressed at six o'clock in the morning, she admitted her project, but refused to attack it in our mutual bedroom. She asked instead if she might borrow my beautiful typewriter from Venice. She would take it downstairs and work in a writing room she had noticed just off the lobby. She left and I went back to sleep.

At a little after nine Sophy, Margie and I looked in on her. We were on our way to the Uffizi Gallery and asked if she were ready to join us. Her mood was gloomy to sullen. She was not ready, she told us. She might never be ready. What had induced her to take on such an assignment as this she could not imagine. Probably she would spend every day in Florence at that desk and never see the Uffizi or the Pitti. She hoped she might be through with it by the time we left for Rome on Tuesday. If, however, she had any better luck than she was having at the moment, she would try to join us at the Uffizi. With the help of a guidebook we established a spot in a particular gallery where we would look for her at half-past eleven.

I could not name, if I were asked, my favorite pictures in the world. And were I to try to make a list of painters I hold in greatest respect, I would have put down El Greco and his ilk, if he has any ilk, at the top of the list. I doubt that I would have included Botticelli. But when in the Uffizi I stood in front of the actual Primavera, I thought with a gasp of surprise that "earth hath not anything to show more fair." And if in my chronicle I seem to have been surprised a good deal of the time, it is because I was. Surprised, and pleased.

We found Zella and that was surprising, too, because the gallery was jammed with viewers, not all of them by any means tourists. There were many family groups from Florence. The reason I know they were from Florence is because I asked them. Father, mother and the children, neatly dressed but in the clothes of working people; they came often, they said, to see the wonderful pictures on days when admission was free. I like to remember those family groups at the same time that I remember the elaborately dressed women at the Opera in Rome. Putting the memories side by side I cannot be critical of the ways in which Italians amuse themselves.

It was about half-past twelve when I left the gallery. Some time before that, realizing that in the crowd the four of us would inevitably become separated, we had arranged to meet around a quarter to one in the square outside. Sophy had noticed when we came in, she said, restaurants with tables and chairs outside where one could order a drink. She had the eye of a hawk for noting such places. We had settled on the nearest one as our meeting place.

As I crossed the threshold of the gallery and came into the square I was rocked by a sound as loud as blasting, except that this was constant; a sort of muffled roar, only not so muffled as I would have liked. To push through it was almost like wading into the surf through actual waves, as the sound beat against me. I saw Sophy almost at once, but when I reached her could scarcely make myself heard. She was seated at a little table.

I bent down and shouted close to her ear, "What on earth is that?" And in the next breath recognizing it, "It's a speech on the radio."

Sophy nodded. I sat down. We leaned across the table toward each other until our heads were nearly touching. It was the only way we could hear each other.

"Look," she said, and pointed up.

I looked where she indicated and saw a cluster of loudspeakers on the top of a post a few feet away.

"All around the square," she said, and I saw she was right.

I have never heard such a thing but I can imagine that if fifty radios within an open area of less than a block were turned on full volume simultaneously, the noise would be something like what we heard that day, particularly if they were not accurately tuned in. This is what made the over-all muffled sound. But above that, or perhaps coming through it, was a political speech, and whoever was delivering it was screaming. I had not heard that kind of delivery since the days when some of Hitler's hysteria was communicated to us over the air.

We ordered Cinzano, but we had to write the word on a piece of paper, and show it to the waiter. He couldn't hear us. And when the Cinzanos came, we couldn't drink them. We were too uncomfortable. My head ached and I felt as if my whole body were vibrating to the sound.

We saw Zella and Margie approaching together, looking at each other and then around the square, their eyes wide, their expression one of acute discomfort and some alarm. We saw Zella point us out to Margie and they reached us on a run. We left money on the table for the waiter and went to meet them.

Sophy anticipated their questions. "Political speech," she bawled. "Let's get out of here."

We found a taxi but we couldn't make the driver hear where we wanted to go. We didn't know, anyway. Our only urge was to get as far away from the sound as possible. Sophy waved her hand forward, and we climbed in the back.

By the time we had gone half a block, the noise had faded a little and we were able to talk, agreeing we had never in our lives heard anything like it, that we felt a little ill, and that we would like to go to Doney's on the Via Tornabuoni. Everyone sooner or later goes to Doney's. Each of us had heard about it for years.

Sophy had no sooner told the driver our destination, than the dreadful screaming noise bore down on us again. We had reached an intersecting street, and looking out we saw on each of the four corners a post like the ones in the square, and on each post a cluster of loudspeakers. This was repeated at every corner on our way to the restaurant. I cannot say that every street corner in the city was wired that day for speeches, because we did not cover the entire city. But from the square to the restaurant and from the restaurant to our hotel, we were not out of reach of that sound. The only place we could escape it was indoors, and I have never been happier to stay under cover.

What we were fleeing, we learned, was the opening of the campaign for the coming elections, but the elections would not take place until the twenty-third of June. This was the seventeenth of May. I had never heard of such a campaigning method as this at home, and I hope profoundly that no one at home hears of the Italian method with enough interest to adopt it.

Doney's Restaurant is actually two, across the street from each other; one a tearoom in appearance, the other a restaurant proper. But the one that looks like a tearoom is where the fashionable world goes for an apéritif before stepping across the street to lunch

in the restaurant. The tearoom in addition to drinks serves tearoom
fare, sandwiches and the like, but this seems to be merely an accom-
modation service. The feature is the bar. The familiars who drink
their apéritifs stand as close to the bar as they can get.

It was crowded when we came in, with men and women, all
of them known to one another, talking back and forth, all of
them fashionably dressed Italians. No Americans. We felt un-
comfortably out of place there and retreated to one of the tables
in the adjoining room. But we did not order sandwiches. We had
each a Cinzano and then crossed the street and lunched at the
restaurant on a delicious cheese omelet. Carts of mouth-watering
food were rolled past us, but wistfully, we let them go by. We
held fast to the pattern we had cut for ourselves at the beginning
of our trip, a slim lunch and a full dinner.

That afternoon we went to the Teatro Della Pergola to see a
performance of Carlo Menotti's *Amahl and the Night Visitors,*
conducted by Stokowski. It was strange, I thought, as I took my
seat, to come all the way to Florence to see for the first time this
little opera that had its première in America, written by a man
I had known slightly when he was a student at the Curtis Insti-
tute in Philadelphia, and conducted by the one-time conductor
of the Philadelphia Orchestra, to whose concerts I had gone on
Friday afternoons.

The opera occupied the second half of the program; the first
was given over to pantomime by two artists, one of these—Marcel
Marceau—the most brilliant I have ever seen. Reading the
program in anticipation, I did not feel I was going to be spell-
bound by such pieces as "Walking Against the Wind" and
"Climbing Stairs." But that was their effect on all of us.

The opera was excellently done and I felt, absurdly, a vicarious
pride in the tumultuous ovation given the composer and conductor.

In the long intermission between the two halves of the program
we walked about in the large foyer, had a lemonade at the bar,

and watched the members of the audience. I thought we were the only Americans among them, but as we were standing at the bar a man and woman came up to Margie and spoke to her by name. Margie instantly edged away from us and maneuvered them a little distance off, talking animatedly with pleasure at seeing them. We recognized the maneuver and the signal it conveyed. We had set it up early in the trip. It meant one of two things, either "These are people from home. I know them but they are spooks. I won't let them become attached to our group, so stay away," or, "I can't remember the name of the person speaking to me. Leave me alone. If I think of it, I'll introduce you."

With these two possibilities in mind, Zella, Sophy and I appraised Margie's companions. Sophy gave a verdict to which we agreed. "Those are very attractive-looking people," she said, "therefore, I'm positive Margie cannot remember their name. Furthermore," she added, "if she could, she wouldn't be acting nearly so cordial."

Margie confirmed this a few minutes later when a bell sounded the end of the intermission. Returning to us, she said, "Those are delightful people. I saw them in Palm Beach last winter and the winter before, and I can't for the life of me remember their name." As we took our seats, she added, half to herself, "I never could remember it in Palm Beach either."

We dined that night in a little restaurant called Da Zi Rosa, Number 12 Via Dei Fossi. I don't know who had told us about this place, but I thank that person with all my heart, for the food we ate, for the music we heard, and for the souvenir from proprietor and staff that I have brought home, and treasure.

There is nothing about the physical aspect of the place, outside or in, to recommend it except its cleanliness. The street on which we found it is narrow and dimly lighted. But as we hunted for the address we were hailed from across the way and asked if we were searching for Da Zi Rosa. We called back that this was our purpose and were enthusiastically welcomed by the man who had hailed us. He was the doorman, and reminded me almost at once of Balieff, that genial master of ceremonies of the Chauve-Souris. I had seen the revue when it was in America many years ago, and I had seen Balieff again as master of ceremonies in the restaurant Maisonette Russe in Paris, but that had been a long time ago, too. I thought of him the moment this doorman greeted us.

The restaurant is long and narrow with tables on either side of a center aisle, and a stairway halfway down. I never learned where the stairway leads. We sat at a table across the room from it and, through an open door that faced us, we could see into the kitchen, busy, and reassuringly neat. At the end of the room by the door through which we had entered, there was a group of musicians, a pianist at his instrument, a violinist with his, and a singer, a young tenor who was in the middle of a song as we entered. We had waited until he had finished before allowing the headwaiter to show us to a table. The young singer was touchingly grateful for this consideration and asked us, as soon as he had finished, if there was anything in particular we would like to hear. Sophy complimented him on his voice and said we would love to hear more music but that we had no particular selections in mind.

The musicians outdid themselves. Barely giving us time to order food and select a wine, the violinist and the tenor were at our table. I am always a little disconcerted when performers in a restaurant give me music at such close range because I can never decide just where to look. But the concert itself was delightful, the violinist of far above average quality, the tenor with a really lovely voice.

We were nearly through our meal when the tone of the program changed. The soloist and violinist rejoined the pianist at the far end of the room. He struck up a gay tune and instantly the Italian "Balieff" popped inside, leaving his post at the door. He snatched up an instrument from the floor near the piano and swept into an astonishing performance on it. From where I sat I could not see what the instrument was. I could make out only that it seemed to have as a base something round that "Balieff" held in the crook of his elbow, and that with his other hand he pumped something like a stick, up and down, as one would manipulate a butter churn. But whatever the instrument was, it was so small, and the man so big, that the instrument was almost completely engulfed by the player.

We had come to dinner late; by this time most of the other diners had left. Looking around me I saw there was only one other table occupied, and its two occupants, a lady and gentleman, absorbed in each other. Accordingly, I ventured to call the headwaiter and asked him if I might be permitted to see the new instrument that had been added to the orchestra.

The proprietor was delighted by my interest. He immediately fetched "Balieff," and "Balieff" came to the table carrying the contraption. The other musicians followed him and our waiter joined them. "Balieff" showed me what he had been playing, and the proprietor explained it. A very simple thing to make, he assured me. You took any kind of round dish or pan, and over it you spread, very tight, a piece of rawhide, tying it down fast, around and around the rim. Then in the center of this taut surface, you made a small round hole, and into this you inserted a long smooth stick, preferably bamboo. To play the instrument you placed a small dish of water beside you and, wetting the fingers of one hand in that, you rubbed them up and down the bamboo stick, holding the instrument curved in the elbow of your other arm. The sound produced was something like that of a muffled drum, but it had its own sound, too, that was not like anything else.

I asked if I might try it. "Balieff" said, "Certainly," and handed it to me. The waiter set down on the table in front of me a finger bowl. I wet my fingers, grasped the drum in the other arm, and set to work. I made the mistake at first of endeavoring to pump the stick, or wand, up and down. But "Balieff" explained I must not do this, I must rub my wet fingers up and down; the wand should remain still.

I caught onto the trick after a minute or two and when the musicians felt I had mastered it, the violinist who was their leader asked politely if I would care to join them in a selection. I was pleased and flattered, and told them so, by saying "*Grazie*" several times.

We gave, I think, a rather fine performance. "Balieff" conducted. My companions applauded it, but happily not one of them asked to try the instrument. I would have been loath to grant permission.

When, some time later, I restored it to "Balieff" I asked the proprietor if it were possible to purchase one. I would like very much, I said, to play it in America. The proprietor repeated that I could make it very easily, but I had to tell him regretfully that in a New York apartment I was not provided with rawhide and bamboo sticks. He could understand, he said, how this might be so, and with scarcely a moment's pause added he would be delighted to have an instrument made for me. I told him how deeply I appreciated such an offer but that, alas, we would be in Florence only one night more. He interrupted eagerly. If we would return for dinner the following night the instrument would be ready.

I answered I could not believe such a wonderful thing to be true. I told him this by saying, "No!"

He assured me indeed it was true and added the pledge of his honor.

I promised we would dine there the following night.

My benefactor asked if perhaps we could come quite late.

We told him we could come very late.

There was a final round of music, "Balieff" executing an hysterical obligato, and at its conclusion, still holding the little vessel under his arm, ushered us out of the restaurant and put us into a taxi.

Monday morning we visited the Pitti Palace and found as much

for wonderment in the furnishings of the great rooms as in the
pictures on their walls. Standing before one after the other of
these, the feeling to which I was almost becoming accustomed
welled up, and I heard myself say aloud, "There it is," to Raphael's
Madonna della Sedia, to his Madonna del Granduca, to his
portrait of Angelo Doni, to a Leonardo, a little farther along a
Velasquez, not long after that a Titian, a Giorgione, a Del Sarto;
on and on, gallery after gallery. The reproductions of these pictures
have passed through the hands of schoolchildren everywhere.

From the Pitti Palace we went to the Church of Santa Croce,
but gave it scarcely more than passing recognition. It is called the
Westminster Abbey of Italy, and the reason for this is evident at
the first glimpse from the doorway of the tombs and monuments
to the Italian great, Michelangelo, Machiavelli, et cetera; almost
ad infinitum.

We lunched at the Grand Hotel and after a brief rest, went in
our car to an address Miss Lelli in Rome had given us. The address
was of the Baroness Renata Rapisardi di S. Antonio. This was on
the card Miss Lelli had given us and underneath it, Villa Palazzo
Bruciato, via Vitt. Emanuele 261 A, Telephone 41164. We had
telephoned from the hotel and had made an appointment with
the Baroness for three o'clock.

The Baroness sells embroidered linens and silks and Miss Lelli
had told us in Rome how this had come about. During the First
World War the Baroness was to be married. The men on her
family's place in the country—it was evidently a large farm—
were all away serving their country. Their wives and families left
behind were in desperate need of money. Nearly all women in
Italy can do fine sewing. They have been trained in this by the
nuns as part of their education. The mother of the Baroness gave
her tenants work by engaging them to make the trousseau for
her daughter: monogrammed sheets, table and bath linens, and
all her underwear. When the trousseau was finished, these peasant
women had begged for more work, and so the benevolent parent

had provided them with material and paid for work in far greater quantity than her daughter could ever use.

By the end of the war there was a considerable surplus of this beautiful needlework. The Baroness spoke of it to her young married friends and they, asking to see it, bought some. That is how it had begun. Word had gone from one to another until the surplus was exhausted, but the demand was greater than ever.

The young Baroness, seeing in this demand an opportunity for giving employment, hunted out once more the women who had made her trousseau. There was scarcely one of those who had not in addition an aunt or a cousin, though perhaps living some distance away, who was a remarkable needlewoman.

Today the Baroness presides over an industry with many workers, each independently working at home, following the patterns and requirements sent by their employer.

The palazzo is behind tall iron gates and at the end of a long gravel driveway. A butler led us up three, or possibly four, flights of stairs. It was, I remember, a long climb to a large room at the very top of the house where the Baroness and her assistant were waiting. All around her, on tables, were piles of the most exquisite needlework I have ever seen: blouses, luncheon sets, dinner cloths, bedspreads, pillowcases in linen, organdy, crepe or raw silk; pink, rose, blue, pale green, lemon-yellow. From the doorway, the four of us, looking, emitted simultaneously a gentle, wistful, envious sigh.

The Baroness was delightful. She spoke English fluently and easily. Her pleasure in the lovely things around her was as enthusiastic as though she, like us, were seeing them for the first time.

We bought blouses, bedspreads, table cloths, pillowcases, ordered monogrammed handkerchiefs, joyfully extravagant.

We had been there about an hour and had almost reached a point of final selections, when Margie said abruptly, "You don't mind if I leave, do you? I'll be outside. I want to get some fresh air."

We didn't mind, and only the Baroness was surprised. Sophy asked Margie if she'd bought anything.

Margie pointed to a neat pile on the corner of a table. "Those are mine," she said. "You give the Baroness my address and let me know how much it comes to. I can pay her downstairs just as well as up here, and I'll have had a little air."

Margie does not walk, she strides. She strode briskly from the room with a charming smile and nod to the Baroness as she passed.

It took another half-hour or so to straighten out our purchases, give addresses for the things to be sent, list monograms for those ordered, and pay our bills. The Baroness came downstairs with us talking animatedly all the way about mutual American friends we had discovered.

The butler joined us at the door and led us out to the car, but there was no sign of Margie. We looked the length of the drive-way to the gate while the butler held open the door of the car for us.

"Your sister is perhaps walking?" the Baroness asked.

"I don't think so," Sophy told her. "She said she'd wait. But I can't imagine where she is."

The Baroness spoke to the butler, asking if he had seen the fourth Signora.

"Ah," he said, and counted us one, two, three. Evidently he had not realized there was one missing, and wondered why we did not enter the car. He answered the Baroness with a shrug of his shoulders. No, he told her, he had not seen the Signora. A lady had gone out some time ago. He had not known she was with us. He had not seen her since he had opened the door for her.

Sophy turned to the Baroness. "May I call her?" she asked.

The Baroness was polite but bewildered. "But certainly," she said. "You think she is hiding, perhaps?"

"You can't tell with my sister," Sophy answered noncommittally. And, raising her voice, called, "Margie!"

Immediately from the upper end of the driveway we saw Margie sit up and then rise from where she had been lying on her back in the gravel. She picked up her mink stole that had served as a pillow, shook gravel from it, waved, smiled, called, "Coming," and hurried toward us.

The Baroness rushed toward her. "You have been hurt? You have fallen down? An accident?"

Margie looked surprised. "Why no, indeed," she said, "why would you think that? I was just lying down. I've had a cold. The sun is wonderful for your sinuses. I loved seeing your beautiful things, and I loved lying in the sun. Do try it. . . . Good-by."

"Good-by," the Baroness echoed. She seemed dazed.

Sophy, Zella and I shook hands with the Baroness and with Margie got into the car. We turned at the gate to wave. The Baroness waved back abstractedly.

"Margie," Sophy asked when we had got well out of sight, "could you tell me why you lay down in the gravel? Couldn't you have gone into the garden?"

Margie evidenced surprise. "Why," she said, "I thought you might not find me there. I didn't want to put you to any trouble."

The shops in Florence stay open until eight o'clock. The moment we had deposited in our bedroom the packages we had brought with us from the Baroness, Zella and I went out for more shopping. I asked her if she thought we were both in the deplorable condition that marks the chronic alcoholic, an inability after two or three drinks to stop. Did she consider that after two or three purchases, that afternoon, we were on a loop?

She said she did, and we set off.

We went straight to the Ponte Vecchio, and if there is a more fascinating place to shop I have never encountered it. For each of my daughters I bought a bracelet of such fineness and delicacy I couldn't believe they wouldn't crush in my hand. They have proven as sturdy as steel bands.

I bought other gifts for my dear ones at home, in leather, in silver; Zella buying at my side. We had a soul-satisfying time, and were so prostrated by the time we reached our hotel again, we slept for two hours.

When we woke, we found Sophy and Margie were in their room but had driven to Fiesole and back. Margie had been to Fiesole on the trip when looking out her window on the Arno had occupied so much of her time. She had dreamed since then of Fiesole as well as the Arno. I hoped her recapture of Fiesole had been esthetically more satisfying than that of the Arno, but I thought it better not to inquire.

As we had promised, we went very late to Da Zi Rosa. It was nearly ten o'clock when we arrived. At the tables we passed, guests were finishing their dinners. Our friends were delighted to see us. We shook hands all around and "Balieff" came from the door to make, with the waiter, a double escort to our table.

Dinner, though we did not repeat the dishes of the night before, was as excellent as the previous one had been, and the musical program just as charming as we had remembered.

When the last alien diner had left the restaurant and we remained the only guests, the proprietor signaled to the musicians. With a flourish they stopped playing and followed where he led them, into the kitchen, calling to "Balieff" who hurried after them, and closed the door to the kitchen behind him.

In perhaps five minutes or less, the procession returned. The door was flung open. The proprietor, at the head of the line, marched toward us carrying between his arms a package as big as a hatbox for a large hat. The doorman was just behind him. The rest, headwaiter, other waiters and musicians, crowded through the door. And all of them circled our table.

The proprietor bowed low and extended the package to me. The waiters sprang forward, removed everything from the table, clear-

ing space for me to place my gift in front of me. The package was well tied; it took a little doing to open. But when I had finally removed the string and paper, I lifted the lid and withdrew my present, holding up for all to see the musical instrument the proprietor had promised and had made with delicate precision, stretching a rawhide tight over a basin beneath. And the basin he had chosen for this special creation was a chamber pot. Concealing the string that held the rawhide taut under the lip of the pot, was a band of bright pink ribbon, tied through the handle of the pot in a crisp and jaunty bowknot. I removed the final wrappings and set it on the table. I didn't know what to say.

No one else spoke, waiting for me.

If these people, I thought, who have been so warm, friendly and gay, have turned out to be vulgar and insulting, I'll cry.

I looked up at them. They were watching me with the anxious, hopeful look of children who make a present at school and, bringing it home to mother, are not sure at the last minute she's going to like it, when they had thought it was going to be wonderful.

Instantly, I knew there had been no insulting vulgarity in their minds, but an eager genuine desire to please and to make me laugh. And that is exactly what I did. I laughed with such relief that my laughter was almost hysterical.

The other grandmothers joined me. Later, each one had admitted she had gone through exactly the same sequence of doubt and reassurance that I had covered.

Our friends, understanding from the laughter that "Mommy" thought the present was dandy, relaxed simultaneously from their tension in one big deep unanimous sigh. That was their last quiet moment as long as we were there. Immediately relief had come to them, they sprang at us, shaking hands with each of us. The owner, exercising his droit de proprietor, kissed the hand of each of us twice round. The musicians ran to the piano. The violinist snatched up his instrument and began to play the instant he had it in his hand. "Balieff," grabbing his mate to my instrument, did not wait for a saucer of water, but spat with glorious generosity on his hand and applied it to the bamboo stick. The tenor expanded his lungs on a high note until we and the walls around us fairly shook. The pianist could scarcely be heard above this volume, but the Lord knows he tried to be.

It was another hour before we could leave, with another round of handshakes to punctuate our reiterations of gratitude for the pleasure they had given us and sorrow at our parting. They remained clustered on the threshold; but "Balieff" escorted us all the way to the corner where he put us in a taxi, bowing low and holding the door open with one hand, and within the curve of his other elbow he nestled his own drum. I carried mine in both hands.

As Zella and I, in bed, put out our lights, Sophy called from the adjoining room. "Emily," she said, "that's going to be a handy little gadget to take with us in the car, and when the customs inspector in New York asks you what it is, what are you going to tell him?"

Chapter 15

THE NEXT morning, Sophy and I paired off for sight-seeing. Zella and Margie went shopping, but separately. I had shopped with each of them and that morning I advised they would not do well together.

Zella's is the direct approach. She shops as she does everything else, rapidly. Her technique is very much like the one she uses in a tennis game, a sport in which she can still trounce opponents far younger than she. She plays with vigor, determination and directness. She has no traffic with subtlety. That is the way she shops. I had been with her when she bought an umbrella for her sister. The instant she had entered the shop and was closing the door behind her, while I at her heels had scuttled to get out of its way, she was saying to the young woman behind a counter, "*Umbrella, per favore.*"

By the time the young woman had come from behind the counter to a rack on which the umbrellas were on display, Zella had discovered it, and had removed three. Immediately I thought of her on the tennis court as I watched her make her selection. She held one umbrella out at arm's length. "I think she'd like that one," she said and laid it on the counter. It was a let ball. "No," she said on the instant she had put it down, "not that one." She held up the second, "Not that one." She looked at the third. "This one," she said, and handed it to the young saleswoman who up to now had taken no part in the transaction.

Margie shops the way my French poodle eats. My poodle approaches his dinner on the rush but the instant he has made contact with the first morsel, drops it, sniffs all around the bowl inside and out, backs away, returns, backs off, walks around the bowl in widening circles, and then leaves the room. A few minutes later he returns, walks around the bowl in narrowing circles until his head is once more over its rim. He then swallows everything in it and asks for more.

I went with Margie to shop on the Ponte Vecchio where I had bought the bracelets for my daughters. She wanted to buy one for a daughter. It is not easy to keep up with Margie's stride. On the last lap I pointed ahead, indicating to her the doorway of the shop to which we were going. When I entered Margie was seated at the counter. The salesgirl brought out four bracelets and spread them on a mat in front of Margie.

"She's the daughter of the owner of the shop," I explained. I had learned this when I made my purchases. "And he makes all these lovely things himself."

Margie found this information and the bracelets fascinating and said so. She selected one, held it up, put it around her own wrist, looked at it again, and said to me, "I don't think I could find anything prettier than this for little Margie, do you?"

I assured her I did not think she could.

Thereupon, she put the bracelet down, stood up, backed off to the doorway, and said to the girl, "Thank you very much. I'll come back later. I want to take a walk now."

That was when I returned to the hotel and joined up with Sophy for sight-seeing and advised Zella to go shopping on her own.

Sophy and I went to the Bargello. Its courtyard and the processional stairway that rises from it are superb. A gallery with open arches above the courtyard is a lovely promenade. But the history of the place is so horrible it is hard to look down from one of these arches without shuddering at the sight of the well in the center below. Originally a palace, the Bargello in 1574 was converted into a prison and place of execution for criminals. The head of the police, the Bargello, officiated here. The torture chamber, the guidebook says, was just off the courtyard where the armory now is. Not long ago, several basketsful of human bones were taken from the well.

But the Bacchus of Michelangelo is here, and masks that he made at the age of fifteen, some lovely Donatellos and, to my considerable surprise, a Mercury. The guidebook said, when I looked it up, it is by Gianbologna. I've seen it since I was a child, on top of an office building on Michigan Avenue in Chicago. The association was so fixed in my mind over so many years, for an instant seeing it so far from home I wondered how it had ever got to the Bargello.

We visited next the Foundling Hospital and saw immediately we left the taxi the row of adorable infants in swaddling clothes that are the Della Robbia medallions. I hadn't known they were on the outside. I stood in some peril on the street delighting in the figures and the blue of the background that is Della Robbia's own shade.

We went in for a minute but only as far as the center courtyard. Through an iron gate at its far end I saw children playing in the garden beyond, and nuns watching over them.

We penetrated deeper than this the Monastery of San Marco, in order to see the Fra Angelica frescoes. They are moving and so is the place itself. We were reluctant to leave and walked several times around the cloisters, neither of us talking very much. It's a quiet spot and I remember almost every detail of it.

At one o'clock, as we had agreed, we went to Doney's. As we got out of the taxi we saw Margie walking up and down outside, getting a little fresh air, she explained when we joined her. We persuaded her to come into the restaurant with us, and Zella joined us a few minutes later. She and Margie were both ex-

hilarated by their successful shopping. Zella had found the Straw
Market and I was cross at having missed it when she described the
bags, hats and even evening skirts she had bought there, each
article, she said, from fascinating people.

Margie disclosed that returning to the shop to which I had led
her, she had bought three bracelets, one for each of her daughters
and a third for her daughter-in-law, and in addition several cigarette lighter-cases in chased silver that is a specialty of the Floren-
tines. By the time she had listed her other purchases there, I had a
suspicion the shop must have closed down at her departure for the
rest of the day in order to restock.

We were weak that day at Doney's. We did not let the carts of
delectable food go by. Instead we took from one, cold lobster, the
sweetest I have ever tasted. I had what a restaurant in Muncie,
Indiana, used to describe as "a perfect gorge."

Immediately after lunch we went back to the hotel, assembled
our bags, sent for the car and took off for Siena with a last look
back at the hammer and sickle that marked our view of the Arno.

Our destination was Siena but about an hour after leaving Florence I began to experience distressing reminders of my "perfect
gorge." Accordingly, I did not see much of the landscape through
which we were passing, but sat back in my corner of the car, my
eyes closed, my arms across my stomach. At one point, however,
opening listlessly one eye, which was as much accomplishment as
I had energy for, I read on a signpost we were at the moment passing "San Gimignano." I yelled, "Halt!" and Sophy very nearly ran
the car off the road.

When she had stopped the machine she turned around in-
dignantly to request that if I wanted to leave the car in order to
lose my lunch, she would be grateful if I would make the request
without scaring the daylights out of her.

I informed her although losing my lunch was my inclination it
was not the purpose of my asking her to stop. "Listen," I said
placatingly, "you remember Edna Welsh at home kept saying

before we left that whatever we did we must go to see 'Jiminy.' "
I explained to the others. "Edna," I said, "never forgets anything
she has seen, but her memory of sound is what you might call not
right sharp. If she can retain one or two of the consonants and
vowels of what she has heard, she lets it go at that, and I'll bet you
anything that 'Jiminy' to her is 'San Gimignano.' And she said it
was absolutely fascinating."

Sophy remembered and was appeased. "Shall we try it?" she
suggested, and we voted yes.

As we went along the road indicated by the signpost, I remembered more and more of what Edna had said. "It has to do with the
Guelphs and the Ghibellines," I told them.

We rounded a curve and I stopped talking abruptly to stare at a
view suddenly revealed. I thought because I was feeling queasy I
must be seeing a mirage. At the top of a high hill that in itself was
startling in the flat surrounding countryside, rose stone towers of
such height I seemed to be looking at an eerie out-of-drawing skyline of New York.

"Look," I said pointing. "Am I seeing what I think I see?" I had
been the first to sight it. The others immediately followed the
direction in which I was pointing. And I was profoundly relieved
to hear them gasp.

"My God," Zella said, "what is it?"

"That," I told them triumphantly as if I had built it myself, "is
San Gimignano. It's just what Edna said it would be." I included
her in the construction of the place.

There are thirteen towers now in San Gimignano, at one time
there were seventy-six. They were built in macabre neighborliness
to one another by members of the Guelph and the Ghibelline
clans. Their proximity was in order for the inhabitants to pour
down boiling oil or sling a few arrows at members of the opposing
clan who might be silly enough to come out into their own back
yard. The neighbors were so active at each other, that the population faced total erasure. So both clans called the whole thing off

and moved to the country. Italy has now made San Gimignano, in toto, a national monument.

We made the inevitable Alpine ascent that marks the entrance to every Italian hill town and came out as always on a piazzo. This one is called the Piazzo Della Cisterna, reasonably enough too, because there is a cistern in the center of the square. There are also two inns, La Cisterna and Leone Bianco. La Cisterna boasts a terrace with a superb view.

We were not there at the proper time for lunch, nor was I in proper condition for a meal. But one day, when I am strong, I will lunch there and I will also climb at least one of the towers. I sat at a little table on the square while the others wandered about and went into the cathedral. And I fell in love with the preposterous place.

We made no further stops and reached the Excelsior Hotel in Siena about five o'clock. I went straight to bed, and the others for a walk. The windows of my room looked down on a stadium and I watched for a time some young men practicing at hurdles, broad-jumps and the fifty-yard dash. After that I fell asleep.

At eight o'clock I woke and found I was sufficiently recovered to join my friends for dinner, though the clear soup I allowed myself was something less than a "gorge."

The girls—we used this term loosely among ourselves—were enchanted with what they had seen and babbled to me excitedly about it. The Campo, they said, is where the famous Palio takes place. I forestalled their condescending explanation of that by telling them I knew the Palio was the famous horse race that takes place in July each year in and around the Campo. It was a great pity we wouldn't be there to see it. I think they were a little crest-fallen to find I knew anything at all, but they perked up and went on to tell me, each one endeavoring to override the others, how fascinating the Campo was, not a square such as we had seen in every hill town, but like an arena, except with little shops of every sort all around its rim, and the center oval-shaped and of an enormous size. They had gone on beyond it all the way to the cathedral square and they said this was a very long walk. But they had been so fascinated by everything they saw, they'd hated to turn back.

Zella repeated a good many times that never in her life had she encountered so many people; not tourists, just citizens, evidently returning from work, unless there was some convention going on. It had been the way it was under the dome in Milan, except that here the rushing, bustling crowd was on every narrow street they traveled.

After dinner we sat a little while in the lounge. Margie picked up an Italian paper from a near-by table. We had been out of touch for so long with what was going on in the world, she said, we had better listen and she would translate for us the events of the day.

The bartender came from behind the bar to join us, and I thank a merciful Providence he did not understand English, because what Margie rendered to us from the Italian would have tossed us and all Americans into prison, placed all Communists in control, and the entire world in the midst of total disintegration. I like to believe this chaos was the result of a personal misunderstanding between Margie and the language, and not the editorial viewpoint of that newspaper.

Next morning I understood and sympathized with Zella's reiterances of the preceding evening. Sophy drove the car in first gear and a series of spurts. But we did reach the cathedral square and parked the car there.

How I love the Siena Cathedral. I walked up and down in front of it. I took pictures of every angle, not that I wanted or needed photographs as reminders, but because I enjoyed looking at it, from this corner and then from the other, then straight on, putting my head back and back to follow the beautiful design all the way up to the top. My normal breathing was not restored by going inside. If anything my gasps came quicker at the sight of the floor, paved in marble and inlaid with scenes from the Bible. Some of this was covered over by the wooden flooring that protects it in the winter, but enough was exposed to give an adequate sense of the wonder of the whole of it.

From the cathedral we went down the street and around a corner to the Baptistery. I confess to being a little disappointed by the famous font there of Della Quercias. Absence of restraint, it seemed to me, was piled on in layers. But perhaps anything immediately after what is my cathedral by choice would have seemed scarcely worth my notice.

I did not pass such judgment, however, on the Campo when we turned into it coming back from the cathedral. The whole wide center area the girls had described to me before as empty, was swarming with people around a shower of tents and booths. This was market day and overnight the folk from the surrounding countryside had set up their wares there.

Margie and Sophy would not allow Zella and me to stop. I daresay they were right. What I saw from the car was so provocative, dusk would have found me still wandering around the stalls. Instead, we drove on at a brisk turtle's pace until we were outside the city limits and the country road open before us.

We reached Orvieto for lunch. The instant we were inside its walls starting the accustomed perpendicular approach to the town proper, we were set upon by boys on bicycles. They rode on either side of the car as effortlessly as if they were on the flat instead of the equivalent of climbing a ladder on wheels, and each sang aloud to us the praises of the hotel he represented. They followed us all the way to the top of the hill and into the square that marked its summit. We told them we wanted first to look at the cathedral, after that we would lunch at the Hotel Palazzo. With good sportsmanship the others cheered the outpost from the hotel we had selected, and left him to wait for us and guide us back to his inn.

I chose Orvieto, too, as a favorite cathedral. Stepping out of the car and looking straight into its face, I reeled with delight at its bright colors that seemed fairly to tumble over one another. The effect of sunlight on them is to make them shift and change like the broken color bits in a kaleidoscope with which children play. Yet for all its gaiety the cathedral has majesty, reaching up with dignity and reverence.

Orvieto, of course, is the place for the wine of that name, and we had it with our lunch. But when we suggested we might like to buy another bottle or so to take away with us, the waiter informed us regretfully but with commendable honesty that Orvieto wine does not travel well. So we came away with only a happy memory of a gentle, fragile wine.

We had scarcely left Orvieto, Margie and I, as always in the back seat, Zella and her map beside Sophy in the front, when Sophy called back to me, "All right, Emily, get out the letter."

"Are we really coming to it?" I asked.

And she affirmed this. "It ought to be fairly soon, now."

While I plunged and groped for the letter in my patent leather knapsack pocketbook, Zella and Margie clamored to know what we were talking about.

Sophy explained. "The day before we left New York," she said, "Ellen and Lloyd Garrison brought us a letter of instructions they had had the last time they were abroad from Berenson, you know the great art authority and scholar. Lloyd had his secretary copy it exactly the way Mr. Berenson had given it to them."

I had brought up from the bowels of my bag a small red leather case that held passport, plane tickets; I had placed this letter there as companion to these treasures.

"Here it is," I said, and opening it read aloud.

Between Montefiasconi and Viterbo you will see on the right hand side of the highway a little sign pointing to Bagnoreggio. Take this road and when you reach Bagnoreggio, which is a little village, motor slowly down the main street until you come to a sort of fork. The left hand side of this fork should be a small road diminishing into a country lane. You walk down this on foot and when you get to the very end—as far as you can physically walk, going always straight ahead of you—you stop and look. What you see will be of large dimensions, so you need not worry about looking for something tiny and obscure. But you will have to keep walking right to the end.

We found the sign to Bagnoreggio and presently the village itself. We followed the main street but we know now you must follow the street itself, not the fork. There is a fork off to the right, and there is a road that branches to the left. Do not take either of these, keep straight ahead, and just as the letter said, you will find the street diminishes into a country lane. You can keep on this in a car until you come to a wide gate that is locked. This is where you leave the car. But someone will come out of a little house on the side of the road and unlock the gate for you. You pass through this and walk across a meadow.

But I will not tell what we saw that day. Others have had a copy of this letter, we have since learned, and no one has given away what, standing at the edge of the meadow, he has seen. You will have to keep walking right to the end. This much I will reveal: You will be rewarded. And I doubt that you will see elsewhere anything like this "Mystery View." It is not recorded on a tourist map.

Chapter 16

THE LAST days in Rome were crowded. For the first time on the trip we felt a sense of urgency to include as much as possible into each twenty-four hours.

Since we were to leave for England on Saturday, we had made no other stop in the car after the wonderful mystery view, and had reached the outskirts of Rome a little after six that same day, Wednesday, May 20.

I doubt that we could have chosen a more unfortunate time. That is the hour when Romans go home from business, and they allow nothing either to stand or to move in their way to that destination. We were honked at, shouted at, grazed by passing motorists and cyclists, and in the confusion lost our way. The traffic cyclone blew us past street corners so we could not mark the signs, past traffic policemen too preoccupied with their own ballet maneuvers to heed our passing cries for help.

In the midst of this, Sophy announced the gasoline tank had registered empty for some time, but she added grimly, "No part of me is going to put a fraction of gas in that tank. I'm going to restore this car exactly as it was delivered to us."

Her purpose was worthy, we agreed, but it did set up in the breast of each of us an added anxiety. If the car actually stopped, we reasoned, it would either be pushed inexorably by the car immediately following, and in whatever direction that car chose, or it was quite within imminent possibility that the cars behind would pile on and over us. Certainly, if three of us got out to push, that is exactly what they would do—pile on and over us.

We went twice around the Vittorio Emanuele memorial that occupies a block, though that course had not been our intention. Once we found ourselves headed at a bridge across the Tiber. The one thing of which we were positive was that the other side of the river was not where we wanted to be, and Sophy sheered off in the nick of time.

But just as the little Fiat gave a hacking cough indicating total dryness within, we rounded a corner, and emerged into our very own street, the Hotel Eden a block away, on a down slope.

We coasted in just as we had coasted off at the beginning of the trip, a perfect balance, as Sophy said. She said it with emphatic satisfaction on the telephone to the man who had delivered the car. "Better bring your friend to help push you down the road to the gas station," she wound up, and was singing when she left the telephone.

By the time we had read the mail that was waiting for us and reread aloud to one another bits of news from our respective children, had bathed and dressed, it was half-past nine when we went out to dinner.

We chose the Restaurant Tre Scalini because it had been recommended to us by friends. We endorse their recommendation. The restaurant is outdoors on a lovely square where children were playing in the darkness, but not noisily, and on benches we could make out dimly the figures of men and women talking, their voices coming through to us softly, from time to time. The food was delicious, and the presence of Ingrid Bergman at the next table with her husband and a group of friends was pleasantly distracting.

Thursday morning, the Princess von Schwarzenburg called for us at ten o'clock. This was the engagement we had made on the day we'd lunched with her before starting on our hill towns trip, and she kept it punctually to the minute. She took us first to the Villa Farnesina and told us on the way that this had been the summer residence of a great banker, an enthusiastic art collector and patron of Raphael. She also told us that as a host he had displayed a little flamboyance but with, at the same time, a pretty wit. In those days, she explained, the road along the Tiber and the protecting walls had not been built. Gardens of villas sloped down to the river. When one dined at the Villa Farnesina it was in a great pavilion on the river bank. The table service was gold and at the end of each course the servants, by training, tossed nonchalantly into the river the plates from which that course had been eaten. But, also by previous training, after the guests had gone, the servants retrieved the plates by pulling in the nets that had been sunk in the river to receive them.

The frescoes in the villa were glorious in one magnificent room after another. This is not included on the usual tourists' list of "musts" and we were enormously pleased to have seen it.

From the Villa we went to the Church of SS. Cosma and Damian. This was the first pagan building to be turned into a church. It was done by Pope Felix IV in about 526 A.D. and it was then that the mosaics for which the church is famous were placed there, and it was for the mosaics Princess von Schwarzenburg had brought us. They are superb. While she was talking to us about them, all of us became aware of a young priest and an old woman standing not far off and looking at the Princess.

Pussy, catching sight of them, interrupted her explanation of the mosaics. "Will you excuse me for a minute?" she said. "The young man is a countryman of my husband's. He's studying here. I'd heard his mother was paying him a visit. They want to speak to me." She left us.

It was touching to see from the old woman's face the pleasure brought by the Princess, and it was heartwarming to see, after the old woman had dropped a deep curtsy and kissed her hand, how

Pussy put them both at their ease, and with what charm she spoke with them.

A few minutes later, the Princess deciding we were not seeing the mosaics in sufficient detail said she had been in the church so many times she was sure she knew how to turn on additional lights. She disappeared behind the altar, and we heard a clicking as if she were trying several switches. She found the one she needed for us and, as the lights came on in the proper place, a door burst open at one side of the altar. A nun came through the doorway energetically and said, loud enough to be heard throughout the church and vehemently enough to cause some alarm, "Who is tampering with the lights? We are all in total darkness."

I may not have got all the words properly, but that was the general idea and it was a pleasure to see the wife of a diplomat caught at a switchboard settle in to diplomatic work. When they parted, the nun was thanking the Princess fervently, I do not know for what.

We drove along the Appian Way, and that is something every traveler should do. Not only to have visions of the men and chariots that have traveled that road, but actually to have concrete evidence and some realization of its length. When we turned back toward Rome I was saying to myself, "This road where Peter asked of the Lord, '*Quo vadis?*', this very Appian Way goes all the way to Brindisi."

We lunched at the Embassy and met for the first time Pussy's husband, the Ambassador. Later, in conference, the grandmothers voted him full marks for charm, ease, hospitality and suitability for Pussy, nodding our heads at each recommendation. American friends were there and it was difficult to leave, because we were having a pleasant time, so that back at the hotel we had barely time to rest a little and change our clothes for a cocktail party friends of Zella's in the American Embassy were giving for us.

Margie was the last one ready but we praised her for delaying because it had brought her out in a costume other than the dark blue gabardine suit. Up to this moment the blue gabardine had been the only daytime costume she had withdrawn from her mound of luggage.

As the doorman opened the door of the taxi for us, Sophy and I promptly and involuntarily executed a sort of minuet step we had learned when entering a taxi that was to contain, also, Zella and Margie. The step was a simple one, just a little backward run on the part of each of us on either side of the door, thereby making an aisle for Zella and Margie through which they could plunge, preliminary to struggling for the privilege of pulling up, opening and sitting on the uncomfortable little seat.

Margie won but Zella, who does not take defeat easily, promptly went around the other side of the car, opened the other little seat, and sat on it. Still Sophy and I waited, with an understanding between us that needed no words.

Margie stepped out. "I think perhaps I'd better . . ." she began.

Sophy nodded. ". . . get your mink stole," she finished for Margie.

Margie was surprised. "How did you know?" she asked. "I did think that if it got chilly, I just might want it." She hurried off.

Sophy and I entered the taxi and sat on the back seat. We would not have dreamed of promoting a second struggle with Margie for the possession of the uncomfortable little one.

"Now," Sophy said, as she settled back, "the question is shall we allow a little extra time for Margie to change her mind once she has the stole, and decide it will be too hot?"

I gave my opinion. "No," I said, "she's better off, I think, in the end with that Excelsior banner of hers. Waving, carrying, or wearing it, she does better than when ruing having left it behind. My idea is keep her from ruing."

When she returned, Margie was wearing the blue gabardine suit, but she kept the stole.

After the cocktail party I went to dinner with an old friend from boarding school, Carolyn Keene, who has a job at the American Embassy, and one of the loveliest apartments in all of Rome. It was good to see her again and though we dined alone, the evening was not without interruption. She owns a cat. Her apartment is high up in an old palazzo and it is the cat's pleasure to roam about outside along the roofs among the chimney pots. In the course of the evening he brought in to us, two salamanders, three crickets and two swallows. Happily, Carolyn was able to restore these, unharmed, to the roof, and after the last one she closed the window.

On Friday Zella stayed alone at the hotel writing her article for the Erie paper. I went back at noon to see if she had finished and could go out. As I opened the door to our bedroom, she looked up from my typewriter and glared at me.

"*You* can't play tennis," she said, "and the chambermaid says *I* look like a movie actress. I've been saying this over and over to myself, but it doesn't help. Go away."

I went away.

But she was with us and in fine spirits, the article posted, when we went to the American Academy for cocktails with Laurance Roberts, its chief. We sat on a rooftop terrace and looked out on a panorama of Rome I shall never forget. I found delightful, too, the story Mr. Roberts told of how the Academy acquired its property. The house had once been occupied by Garibaldi. It had passed into the hands of an old lady who in turn had willed it to the Academy, but her heirs had contested the will because she'd also left money to her pet donkey. Eventually, however, benefactors had made possible the purchase of the property, and it is now undisputably the Academy's own.

We dined again at Tre Scalini. We are not ones, we agreed that night, to be flirtatious with food. It means too much to us. When we find a good restaurant we are faithful to it.

Saturday was our last day in Rome and only a half-day because our plane for London was scheduled to leave at 3:15 P.M. We left the hotel early and spent the entire morning at the Baths of Caracalla. There were other places to which we had wanted to pay farewell homage, but we were unable to leave the Baths, partly because of the fascination of that extraordinary place, and partly because we were in the inexorable hands of a guide. The guide had attached himself to us on our arrival. We had tried to shoo him off, and he had responded in exactly the pattern of a slap-happy puppy who is determined to be wanted.

In the beginning we'd said, "No, thank you," very politely. He stayed with us.

A few minutes later Sophy said more firmly than the first time, "No guide, thank you."

He smiled, and drew our attention to the way the Romans had drained off water in the steamroom. As we walked on he yapped cheerfully and steadily. We tried ignoring him but he continued to frisk about us.

Finally, exasperated, I turned on him, stamped my foot, waved my arm and shouted, "Go away!"

He stood for a few minutes in the spot where I had challenged him, but when we had moved a few yards ahead, he trotted after us and, keeping a few feet behind, continued to yap. That was our last stand. In a few minutes he had edged up and was with us once more. We gave in, and he took over.

In very little time he had us where he wanted us, underneath the Baths by way of dank, damp steps. It was an eerie place, staggering in size, in a grotesque way like an area that has been marked off for a real estate development, the houses not yet put up, but the roads in, except that this whole area was of course covered. The passages that were as wide as roads bent around enormous pillars that supported the structure above, and crossed other roads, turning and twisting so that I felt a claustrophobic panic. If that frolicsome puppy who was leading us, I thought, should consider it a prank to desert us, we might wander around and around down there until we died. Perhaps years later our bones would be discovered and treasured as relics of early Christian martyrs.

I clutched Zella's arm and, borrowing Mélisande's words, hissed in Zella's ear, "I am not happy here."

But Zella said, "S-s-s-hh," impatiently. She was listening to the guide who before my eyes had changed from an irrepressible puppy to a wicked sprite.

He was explaining with vivid pantomime that this dreadful place we were in was where the slaves had worked and lived, forbidden to go aboveground and enter the rooms overhead.

"That's us," I said to myself. It was a melancholy thought. As I plodded along I pictured how it was going to be down there, and then wondered if I should grab the guide's arm and hold onto it with both my hands to prevent his abandoning us, would the purpose of my attack on him be misconstrued? Before I had resolved this idea into action the guide, rounding a bend that was certainly the twentieth we had rounded, revealed to us a passageway wider than any we had traveled. It was an avenue, and by God's mercy I could see light at one end of it.

This was the place our leader had wanted us to see. It was for the privilege of standing on this spot that he had attached himself to us, and as he explained this I saw him transformed back to his former guise, anticipating a pat on the head. He looked wistfully from one to the other of us, begging our approbation. This was the road, he explained grandly, set aside for members of the American Embassy and other diplomatic corps, to travel in their cars when they came to the concerts held during the summer in the Baths above. Was this not, he wished to know, both generous and ingenious of the Italian Government to provide such a passageway and remove from our representatives the inconvenience of public traffic?

I had not come to the Baths of Caracalla in order to see a private entrance to a parking lot, but I was so thankful for light in my vision ahead that my appreciation of the government's thoughtfulness was hysterically enthusiastic.

The sprite took possession of the puppy once more when safely aboveground Sophy tipped him for the services we had not wanted. The sum was inadequate he told her fiercely—his was a fixed charge with a little added for courtesy. But when she had granted the money he demanded, he was his jolly self again. In a final spurt of attachment to us, he wrested Zella's camera from her hands and photographed the four of us, commanding us to laugh as he directed. That turned out to be the best picture Zella got from her camera.

A bus took us and our luggage from the hotel to an office in the Quirinal Hotel where plane travelers assemble for the weighing of their luggage, checking of tickets, et cetera. In Rome this is not done at the airport but at a downtown center, and the bus for us was an unusual service that I maneuvered and that cost me lunch with the others at the Capriccio. I had to stay behind.

"If only you didn't have ideas," is a tedious refrain my friends had repeated with monotonous frequency during the trip. However, from this idea we did get a bus ride.

Early that morning, the day of our departure, a gentleman from BOAC had telephoned me. "Miss Kimbrough," he had said in a bright, cheery voice, "I want to welcome you to Rome and to ask what we can do to make your stay here pleasant."

I was somewhat taken aback. "Why, thank you very much," I said, "we're leaving today."

"Dear me," he answered, "you are making a very brief visit, aren't you?"

With my customary subtlety I gave him back, "Why no, we came two weeks ago." It was at that instant I had my idea and since it is customary for me to convey an idea simultaneously with having it, I continued with, "You *could* do something for us, as a matter of fact, for which we would be very grateful. We have, that is one of us has, a considerable amount of luggage. I don't know how we can get it and ourselves in taxis to your office, where I understand we have to stop for checking. I would appreciate it very much if you could send a car for us, except that we'll need more than one."

There was a slight pause and then the voice told me this could of course be arranged, but the details would have to be conveyed to me later. Would I receive a telephone call at some time during the morning?

I said we were going out but would be back by noon and I would be receptive then to telephone calls. That was why when the others went off for lunch I, between gulps of progressively chilling omelet in the Eden dining room, took telephone calls in a dark booth off the lobby.

The first call was from a secretary of the BOAC office. She said she understood I had asked the use of the manager's car to take myself and friends from the hotel to the central office. There was a little difficulty about securing that because it had gone to the country, taking the manager's family. It had been sent for but there was some question about its returning in time. Would I consider a substitute?

We got that cleared up, I thought, and I returned to my omelet.

The next call was from another secretary who repeated the message of the first, adding the entreaty that I content myself with the car of the assistant manager. I straightened her out, too, but by this time I had a vague doubt in my mind of the solid gold worth of my original idea.

The third, fourth and fifth calls took me through the motor equipment of lesser officials of the company with an offer to me and my friends of all of it. My answer to each of these was a request to skip the whole thing. All we wanted were taxis or a bus— any means of getting from one place to another—and we would ourselves take care of the getting.

The sixth call was a triumphant announcement that all had been arranged. Would we be ready at a quarter to two? We would be ready, I promised, and returning to the last vestige of stone-cold omelet, I ordered a glass of wine.

I had no sympathy from my friends when they returned from a warm, nourishing lunch, only a tiresome repetition of the refrain about me and my ideas.

Our conveyance, that arrived promptly at a quarter to two,

was a chartered bus. It turned out to be not excessive. Margie's luggage occupied a good quarter of it. Zella personally effected considerable displacement because in order to maintain her

superior rating of three bags, she wore draped about herself a motley collection of knapsacks, made respectively of twine, imitation leather that smelled, canvas, and a plastic substance that crackled. Ordinarily a figure of superbly straight carriage, she looked, when standing with these flying buttresses attached to her shoulders and belt, like bent fishermen I have seen in pictures titled, "Bringing Home the Nets."

As we drew up in front of BOAC's central office I saw from the window of the bus my dear friend, Carolyn Keene, standing on the pavement. I knew she had come to see us off and was touched. However, at the sight of our vehicle and us and our luggage descending from it, though the odd lots we were carrying in hand could never have been classified as luggage, she hesitated and I saw her half turn away. But one of Carolyn's dearest qualities is her staunch loyalty to a friend. She turned back, came over to us and openly acknowledged her association by shaking each of us by the hand. The four of us will be grateful to her for all time and to the Providence that bestowed her with a gift of loyalty stronger than her sense of embarrassment, because without her fluent Italian we might never have reached London and seen the Coronation.

How the gentlemen at the weighing-in desk made their computations, I do not know. I have always thought that the principles of mathematics were the same the world over, but since I have never grasped any part of those principles, it would be presumptuous of me to make any assumptions about it. However, sub-normal as I am when asked to manipulate X and Y into an equation, I can detect a mathematical oddity in an assessment of $109 excess for Margie's luggage, but $45 divided among the four of us if we wished to pool our pieces. It was one thing, however, to note this discrepancy and quite another to convey it in Italian across the counter to its perpetrators. Of all the numerals the one with which I have consistently had the greatest difficulty in Italian is five, and its multiples.

At this point Carolyn entered the conversation. Nothing in Italian nor about Italians is difficult for her. While she was bringing the mathematical discrepancy to a level, with equal fluency she was soothing a line of passengers, mostly Italian, behind her, Sophy, the banker, went to the cashier's window and there her troubles began. She wanted to cash American Express checks to an amount of lire that would dispose of them and leave us with no excess on our departure. But she had no sooner extracted a check of a denomination nicely to achieve this lack of leftover balance, than I, a courier, brought a message from Carolyn that the gentlemen were changing the assessment. The changes rose and fell with a rapidity and divergence that would have brought the stock market to collapse, and reduce me to breathlessness, carrying the good and the bad news from Carolyn to Sophy.

I brought the final message a second too late. Sophy had cashed a check that left her with a residue of three thousand lire. She was not happy about this, but she joined the rest of us in hurried but fervent phrases of gratitude to Carolyn that continued until, in the ordinary bus provided for all passengers, we had been driven out of her hearing.

At the airport three of us stood in the waiting room. Zella put as much of herself and her dangles as was possible on a bench that had partitions at intervals to accommodate an ordinary seat. The plane was due to leave in a few minutes. Margie moved away from Sophy and me and began to walk in her characteristic stride back and forth and around the room. Sophy and I joined Zella. We knew how difficult it had been for Margie to decide to fly with us to London. She had flown once, some twenty years before, and had declared then and persistently since, that she would never fly again. She was breaking this vow in order to be with us, but we in turn were not willfully inflicting such distress. I had to be in London by Monday because my daily broadcasts would start that afternoon. To go by train would have cut short our time in Italy and we had treasured every minute there.

"Margie's really an awfully good sport, isn't she?" Sophy said. "She's as nervous as a cat, but she's going to go through with this."

Zella's answer was she had been thinking just that, and how wonderful Margie was.

I asked tartly if anyone had happened to notice how wonderful

I was and what a good sport. After all, I'd told them often enough, I said, how much I hated flying.

There was a conspicuous lack of response to this from my friends.

Sophy's only comment directed to Zella was, "At least she doesn't talk when she's on the plane."

"That makes *me* nervous," was Zella's astonishing reply. "Nineteen hours on the plane coming over, and not one word out of her. That would scare anybody to death who knows Emily."

A young man in a smart uniform and smiling gaily spoke from the middle of the room. "May I have your attention, please?" he said. "Passengers for flight number *something* or other [this was ours] to London, a slight engine trouble has developed, and there will be a delay in the takeoff. We are not at this moment able to tell you how long the delay will be. An extra engine part is being flown to us from London should it be required. In that event the flight may have to be postponed until tomorrow. Should this be necessary the company will arrange hotel accommodations for all passengers and provide transportation back to the city. Will any passengers who wish to avail themselves of this, please come to the desk? Will the others wait here for a further report? Thank you very much."

I felt as if I had been invaded by field ice, if that is what the ice that moves is called. This was moving around me, mostly in my stomach. "Laughing about it," I said aloud, "That's what you get with airplane people. I never heard a train announcer laugh."

Margie had stopped walking at the young jokester's first words. She came over to us when he had finished. She, Zella and I turned to Sophy, leader of our little band.

"Well," she asked, "what do you want to do? Shall we go back to town and see if we can get our rooms again at the Eden?"

"If I go back," was Margie's answer, "I'll never come out here again, I know that."

I was with Margie every inch of the way back and not at one inch to return, and I said so.

During the entire trip Zella's platform had been, "Whatever the rest of you decide is fine with me." She had a surprise for us. "Whatever the rest of you decide," she began, and we smiled at the familiar generous refrain, "I am staying right here and flying to London," she ended.

It gave us a jolt, me particularly.

"Well," Sophy answered after a pause that had allowed us to believe what we had heard, "I think you've got the right idea. Suppose we go back to the hotel and the plane takes off? I don't think we'd have a prayer of getting on another one tomorrow."

We discussed it back and forth a little longer, but Zella's emphatic declaration had really decided us. We were still discussing, however, when Margie interrupted. "I'm going to get some fresh air," she announced and strode off, disappearing through a door at the far end of the waiting rom.

Sophy suggested finding a restaurant bar. She was sure there would be one. Zella agreed enthusiastically, readjusted her dangles and went with Sophy. I followed them silently. I was back with my field ice again.

When Margie found us a few minutes later we were seated at a table in a restaurant, but we hadn't ordered anything. No one had asked us to. It was four o'clock and we couldn't think of anything we wanted to order. We were just sitting.

"There's the most beautiful promenade deck above," Margie reported. "The sun is shining, the air is wonderful. Why don't you come up?"

"Dearie," Sophy told her earnestly, "it's an absolutely heavenly, golden day. Perfect flying weather. Just remember that. It makes all the difference."

Sophy had flown to India two years before, and this put her knowledge of flying in our estimation, on a par with Rickenbacker's. "Believe me," she went on, "it's not pleasant to go off

in rainy weather. But honestly, darling, they won't let us go unless
the engines are all right. And with the weather as perfect as this,
you don't need to worry."

Margie made a pretty good showing of a smile. "Of course not,"
she answered. "I'm going back," and left us.

Half an hour later she returned, her steps from the door to our
table were even longer than her usual stride, and she began talking before she had quite reached us. "There's the largest, blackest
cloud I've ever seen in my life coming right toward us. And it's
getting very windy."

I looked for the first time out one of the windows of the
restaurant. Pieces of paper were swirling in the air. I pointed
toward the window. "It's windy," I said.

Margie, Zella and I looked to Sophy for comment. We had it.
"Let's order a drink. Thank God we've got that three thousand
lire left over."

Margie glowered at her sister. "How can you think of such a
thing at a time like this?" she demanded. She left us.

Sophy, looking after her, observed contemplatively, "This is a
moment to remember. Margie refused a drink. She must believe
she is facing the end." Sophy, who drinks only sherry, Cinzano,
or wine, ordered a double Scotch.

I drank some hot tea but got no thawing effect from it. Zella
had a Cinzano and talked gaily and brightly as she sipped it.

The restaurant was not full. Other passengers, we conjectured,
must have decided to go back to Rome. People who remained were
not talking much. As I watched them I saw one after another
look toward the window and then quickly back into the room
again. I looked frequently, too, though I tried not to. There was
no sunlight and it was perceptibly darker than it had been half
an hour before. Windier, too.

The rain came about half-past five, a cloudburst. I walked over
to the window. The drops made holes in the loose sandy soil. I
saw Margie, head lowered, hurrying down the stairs from the

promenade deck. Her coat was wrapped around her legs by the wind. I joined her at our table.

"Have a drink?" Sophy asked.

"Certainly not," Margie answered.

Sophy ordered another.

Nothing that had happened up to this moment scared me as much as this. Sophy putting down two double Scotches was unmistakably giving a sign that she was caving in from fright. Sophy the stalwart, the impregnable. The substances of which we two were made, I would have said, were as granite to pale lemon sherbet, and I would as soon have conceived of Gibraltar, as Sophy, turning to my substance.

The young Sunny Jim who had made the first announcement brought another message into the restaurant. He was as merry as a grig. "The engine has been repaired," he told us. "The plane will leave in less than an hour."

I didn't hear what else he said. I was on my feet talking to my friends. "I've had enough," I warned them. "I'm going to telephone. I'm going to get the American Express and any other travel agency I can think of. I'm going to get us on a train. I wasn't meant to fly." I didn't wait to hear what the others said.

As I left, Zella called after me, "Whatever the rest of you decide, I'm going to fly."

I even heard Margie's answer, because it was loud. "You've said that eight times, Zella."

I had not reckoned nor wrestled with placing a call over an Italian telephone. It is not a simple process. Standing in a little booth, sweating on the outside though my vitals were still icebound, I found the names I needed in the telephone book, translated the numbers into Italian, and yelled them into the telephone. I got no answer from the American Express or from Thomas Cook. I called the Eden. I talked to my friend the porter. Those offices I had called, he reminded me pleasantly, were closed. I asked him for train information and he gave it. The significant item in it was that, computing from the time he could get us, perhaps, accommodations on a train to the time we would reach London, we would do almost as well by oxcart. I pondered the relative importances of how I felt, and how I would explain to CBS missing the first two or three days of broadcasting.

The door behind me was pulled open and Sophy bawled in my ear, "They've called the plane. Do you want to go or not? You'll have to decide quick!"

"*Grazie*," I said into the telephone, "*e arrivederci*. I'm going to fly."

What had been holes in the sand had become puddles to the ankles when we stepped outside. A bus was drawn up as close as it could get to the portico. We were requested to board it. So we splashed through only a few of the puddles, but the rain was so heavy, we could not walk to the plane, though that was only perhaps fifty yards away. We were delivered to the foot of the ramp and at the very second Margie and I walked up it, a clap of thunder came, and Gabriel's trumpet will not be louder. A zigzag of lightning parted the sky right up to the throne itself, was my estimation before I shut my eyes and wavered the rest of the way up the ramp and into the maw of the plane.

The flight was dazzlingly beautiful. We rode high but between two cloud levels. It was strange to see nothing but clouds below and at the same time only clouds above. But those above were of every delicate shade and we were in sunlight. Not that I looked much. I had the book of Double-Crostics out of my bag before I'd fastened my safety-belt. It was Margie who forced me to glance up and out.

I sat with Sophy. Zella's seat was across the aisle and the place for Margie beside her. But Margie was not in it more than a few minutes at a time. The plane was not full. Some passengers, as we had surmised in the restaurant, had gone back to Rome. Margie took advantage of the empty seats. She played "Going to Jerusalem" up and down the plane. Part of her excitement was, of course, an outlet for her nervousness, but also she was transported by the beauty outside, and she looked at it from every window she could reach and insisted on the attention of each of us to everything she saw.

When I was made to look out, I noticed a shimmer of light that moved down the nose of the outside engine. "That's the sunlight touching the metal," I thought to myself. "If it looks like drops of oil to me, that's because I'm such a fool I let myself imagine these things." Therefore I made myself look at it each time Margie prodded me and tried to think how pretty it was.

The steward was courteous and attentive. Serving us our dinner trays he directed Sophy's and my attention to the way the pilot was giving us a smooth passage. "Taking us a little out of the way, of course, but you see how he avoids those storm cloud bunches, like making a detour in a car, you might say."

When we came out of the clouds the sky around us was clear, and below us we saw lights. As we were fastening our safety-belts for the landing, our steward came back to say he hoped we'd had a pleasant trip. I asked him what the trouble had been that caused our delay.

"Why," he answered, "it was an oil leak in that engine over there." And he pointed to the one I had watched.

But the wheels of the plane had touched the ground. We were on the landing field. We were rolling toward the depot, and we were in London.

Chapter 17

B ARBARA'S HOUSE in London is on a quiet square and in the center of the square there is a charming little green park. Because of the postwar housing shortage, Barbara has had made into apartments the top floors and rented these, keeping for herself only two bedrooms. There were four of us and a fifth grandmother, Marian Boyer, was flying over from Philadelphia and due the day after our arrival. In the mews, the street that ran for a block behind this and the neighboring houses, there is a little apartment for guests that overflow the main house. It can be reached either through the garage or outside, by walking round the corner. Zella, Sophy and I chose the apartment. We told Margie firmly she and Marian were far more susceptible than we to luxury and, provided with it, would diffuse a happier spirit over the group than we might expect from them under plain surroundings. Margie declared this a slur on her lovely equable nature but after one look at the accommodations proffered her, accepted the slur since, she said, such a beautiful big bathroom came with it.

We loved our apartment the instant we reached it but that in itself was not easy. The stairway that led to it was almost as steep as a ladder placed upright and so narrow that to avoid getting stuck on the turn, it was safer to make the ascent on the bias. The apartment itself included a sitting room with a tiny fireplace, a little kitchen, two bedrooms and a bath but the arrangement of these was eccentric. The occupant of one bedroom had to go through the other in order to reach the bath and the W.C. was an independent unit in the hall, enclosed, however. By drawing lots, Sophy and I shared the double bedroom. Zella had one to herself but it was small and it was she who had to travel across our room in order to reach the bath. There were other oddities, too. The plumbing of the W.C. at haphazard intervals, never when in use, emitted either a falsetto titter that reached every corner of the apartment or a lugubrious wail equally penetrating. Water for the bath was heated from a little machine over the kitchen sink. It was disconcerting to enter the tub absentmindedly without a preliminary visit to the kitchen because turning on the hot tap produced a forceful stream of cold water. On the other hand, the little machine worked with such rapidity that in only the length of time required for the return to the bathroom after pushing the lever in the kitchen, very hot water shot out of the tap into the tub. I do not understand to this day how such a thing could be, but it was. On the night of our arrival Cameron showed us its accomplishments and tucked us into our beds.

Cameron was one of three maids who had welcomed us when we had stumbled into the house at half-past eleven at night, giddy from exhaustion. Though they had expected us before seven and had had no message, they had waited up for us with hot soup and a cold supper ready. We had eaten ravenously, admitting sheepishly to one another that somehow we had not had much appetite for dinner on the plane, though Margie had protested she'd not wanted to take the time from looking at the view. After supper, we had toured the house under Cameron's guidance, bestowed Barbara's own bedroom and bath on Margie, and, led by Cameron, gone with our bags through the basement passage, heaved them and ourselves up the ladder stairs, been shown by Cameron the ways of our own apartment, and been put to bed. All this in two hours from the moment of our arrival.

At nine o'clock on Sunday morning, when we woke, we were happy to find our faculties considerably sharper than they had been when we had gone to bed. We were hazy about the workings of the hot-water heater but Sophy, getting breakfast, inadvertently pushed the lever above the sink thinking dimly that Cameron had said this would light the stove. She very nearly parboiled Zella who was taking an invigorating cold tub. I was in the kitchen, too when this happened, cutting a grapefruit, and Zella's Comanche yell and wild-eyed gallop into the kitchen very nearly cost me the tip of a thumb. But they also recalled instantly to my mind Cameron's demonstration of the machine the night before. Sophy remembered it simultaneously and we both thanked Zella for reminding us.

The vocal idiosyncrasy of the W.C., however, wakened no recollections in either of us. It was a total surprise and Zella, again, was its victim. She was walking past the little cubicle when the sound came, and in one magnificent leap collided with Sophy and me rushing to the scene from opposite ends of the apartment. The three of us with fearful wonder looked at and listened to the contraption. Zella asked, with reason, if Sophy had been tampering with anything else in the kitchen and added a suspicion that the "john" was going to blow up and take us with it. As Sophy was denying vehemently any part in it, the tittering died away. And since its performance had stirred no memory in us of any warning the night before, we came to the conclusion Cameron's gentility had prevented her mentioning it.

We went over to the main house by the outside way, walking to the corner along our mews and just around it up the front steps. The door was opened for us by one, who was not Cameron, of the three maids that had welcomed us so comfortingly the night before. By the light of our restored faculties and because we asked her, we were able to identify her as Ruth, the parlor maid. We also learned from her the cook's name was Winnie and that she was in the kitchen. The kitchen was in the basement. She was expecting our orders for the day. Would we ring when we had made our plans?

By the same means that had identified Ruth, we oriented ourselves in the house. The dining room was on the first floor, to the right of a wide center hall. On the left, Ruth told us, was a room her ladyship had turned into a studio where she displayed the pottery that she made.

"She's turned into a lovely artist," Ruth boasted, "makes it all herself, too, in an oven in the garage."

Later we saw Barbara's kiln.

We went up a broad stairway at the end of the hall. From windows on its landing we were abashed to discover we could see directly across a narrow alleyway a row of our own toilet articles on a shelf in our bathroom in the mews.

On the second floor, we looked again at the rooms we had been too heavy-eyed to notice the night before. The one above the dining room was a drawing room. Seen in the morning light, it was lovely. From the night before I had taken in the impression only that there was a piano in it. We had eaten our supper on a little table in front of the fire in a library across the hall. Supper had been the only thing here that had interested me. Now I saw its French windows opened on a balcony and standing on it, I looked down on a little green park. The day was was sunny, the air warm. The library itself was a delight, with books to the ceiling, pleasant comfortable chairs, a large writing table.

I didn't look further. On the writing table were little stacks of mail and on the top of one of these stacks was a letter to me in the handwriting of one of my children. I snatched my pile with happy cries and Zella and Sophy each pounced on hers. Clutching our treasures, we hurried out of the room and down the hall, calling to Ruth we would see the lady upstairs and then let Cook know the plans for the day.

We found Margie dressing in her bedroom. At the sight of us, she endeavored hastily to throw her wrapper over a breakfast tray, muttering shamefacedly that Cameron had insisted on bringing it to her. We were loftily magnanimous. Sophy assured her we much preferred our little flat and doing things for ourselves to indolent lolling. We were completely happy, I corroborated, where we were. Zella vouchsafed a few qualifications to this over-all happiness but admitted she did not expect these to be repeated.

Sophy reminded Margie it had been planned long ahead to drive to Oxford on this Sunday and lunch with their cousins. Did Margie still want to go? If she felt tired, Sophy must telephone the cousins and let them know. Margie was not tired, wouldn't think of disappointing the cousins, was dying to drive to Oxford, it was a beautiful day. She was still delivering these insistences when we left her; Sophy interrupting her only to say we'd wait in the library and that there was mail there for Margie.

We had a short and impromptu business meeting on the way back to the library. The outcome of it was that Sophy was elected to give orders and run the household since she was to continue as banker. Clinching this appointment, I said I saw no need for any of the rest of us to feel Sophy was being imposed upon because we all knew she liked it, nor any need for Sophy to relinquish her position of importance since none of us wanted it and she'd be unhappy at giving it up. There was no further discussion.

In the library Sophy rang for Cook, told her we would be out for lunch and in for dinner, and asked her to bake one of the hams we had shipped from New York in advance of our coming. Ruth was told to expect Mrs. Boyer sometime during the day and to explain to her we were sorry not to be in when she arrived, but had gone to Oxford for lunch. Preening a little and endeavoring not to show it, I told Ruth I was expecting a car that would take us to Oxford. Would she let us know when it arrived? I thought it unnecessary to explain to her that a car and chauffeur were being provided for me by CBS during my stay in London, and though this was elevating me to a style to which I was totally unaccustomed, the purpose for which this was being provided was not style but a practical way of making sure I gathered in the greatest possible amount of material for my broadcasts.

We settled down to our mail and had a happy tearful time over it, when Margie joined us. We allowed her only a little cry over hers because the car was waiting.

I had never seen hawthorne hedges in bloom before that drive, and how many times I had read about them in English poetry! And laburnum in full feathery cloud of yellow. The meadows were a shining, glistening green, the trees in full leaf, the lilacs were out. I had not been in England for more than twenty years and I had never been there in the spring. As we say in Indiana, "I like to have died over it."

Dr. and Mrs. Lee were at the gate when we drove up to their house in Oxford. And though they are not tall people, the branches of a laburnum tree in an exultant sunburst of bloom almost touched the tops of their heads. Dr. Lee is a distinguished scholar, a Fellow of All Souls College, and the only man equipped and privileged to practice law in three continents—England, Canada and South Africa. He stoops a little; his build is slight, his eyes the blue of Delft china, and he frequently does a sort of trick with them. Seeming to be asleep because they are closed when he is listening to conversation, he suddenly opens them as if he were using that startling disclosure of bright blue as an exclamation mark to punctuate what he has said.

Mrs. Lee is shorter than he, and plumper. Her store of knowledge is not from the law books on his shelves. It comes from poets, essayists, novelists, and is "the best butter." She uses quotations as punctuation, emphasizing an observation of her own with something of Ruskin or Matthew Arnold. Her range is wide and her memory of an accuracy and scope to make me weep with despair that mine contains only little snatches of what I once read and knew. She and Dr. Lee had been in America the preceding year visiting Sophy and Margie's father. I had met them then and they had come as guests on my program. I had been looking forward since the beginning of the trip to a reunion with their warmth and gaiety. And they gave them to us in such generous hospitality as to make even Zella, whom they met for the first time, feel she was a guest they particularly liked having there.

After lunch, we made a little tour of the house, since the house itself is not large. But it cannot be toured hastily because there is so much in it to see. A beautiful Italian primitive over the fireplace in the living room, purchased many years ago on a trip to Italy—and we heard the story of that—souvenirs of other trips abroad, photographs and keepsakes of relatives mutual to Mrs. Lee and Margie and Sophy, the books in Dr. Lee's study that crowded shelves rising to the ceiling—how familiar to me the whole house was. Not that I had ever been in it before, but houses in English novels are all like this one. The size varies, but not the details: family photographs, keepsakes, souvenirs of travel, walking sticks in the hall.

I heard Mrs. Lee say to Sophy, "There, dear, on the desk are the photographs I've written you about in my letters. And that clock over there I've written about, too. And you heard it ticking, you remember, when your family telephoned us on Christmas Eve. How exciting that was, and I made Robert stop the clock before it should strike—the only time it's ever been stopped. When we had it as a wedding present, dear me, we never thought one day it might interrupt a telephone call all the way from America."

As I listened to her I had an idea about a particular quality that seems to me to be common to all English writers, that is, their awareness and communication of detail. I thought about Mrs. Lee writing letters to her family in America and putting into them all the trivia of photographs on the desk, the clock ticking, things most Americans would not include in their messages from home to members of their family away. And perhaps that was because most American families do not have members living in distant parts of the world. But English families are separated by the very nature of the Empire that we must learn now to call the Commonwealth. Colonization demanded that colonizers go out from a home base, but they had never become entirely separated from that base because of just the sort of letter Mrs. Lee writes. Year after year, mothers in England had written such letters to sons and daughters in India or wherever, reminding them of the photographs on the desk, the walking sticks in the hall, something blooming in the garden, the wallpaper in a bedroom that was fading a little. Boys in England go away to boarding school at a much younger age than we send ours. To lessen their homesickness, mothers have written about the simple familiar things they had left. Therefore, they've all been conditioned, as a psychiatrist would say, to an awareness and appreciation of the details of their environment. And so, those of them who took to writing included this as a matter of course. The British writer is an honor graduate of a correspondence school of writing.

Endeavoring to communicate to the rest this idea with which I was pleased, I solicited the attention of the group. I didn't get it. I dare say that is why I have written here my conjectures.

We sat in the garden a little while to look at a lovely hawthorne tree there. Mrs. Lee wanted us to have some time with it before we saw All Souls. All afternoon, Sophy and I took pictures. Zella was at outs with her camera and had left it in London. Each time Sophy or I clicked the shutter, Mrs. Lee gave a happy cry of wonder at our skill, and delight in the snapshots she could add to her collection.

Oxford, I think, cannot be more beautiful at any time than it was that afternoon in the soft warm sun. On the way home, in the car, when we had dropped Dr. and Mrs. Lee at their house and said our good-bys, we admitted to one another each of us had experienced a considerable satisfaction in being taken into places that could be entered only by a Fellow. Doors had been unlocked by Dr. Lee with a key he carried on his watchchain and we told Zella she had been nothing less than inspired when she had asked him in his study to put on his scholar's robes. He had done it shyly and protesting. But the moment he had adjusted them and turned to face us, the sun had come in a dusty slanting shaft, across his face and down one shoulder of his gown. We said we'd remember that.

Marian Boyer was at the house when we reached home. She'd arrived a few hours before, had had a bath, a nap and was full of talk and so were we. Marian is small. Her hair is red, her eyes are blue and she dresses with such fastidiousness and chic as to make it impossible to picture her emerging from anything but the proverbial hatbox—hers probably lined with mink. Actually she has lived in the jungle on archaeological digs. She has run an important museum while its head was at war, and she is the mother of four children, the grandmother of close to twelve. She had been a friend, for many years, of Margie's, Sophy's and mine, but Zella had never met her. Within a quarter of an hour of their meeting they had discovered innumerable mutual friends. By bedtime, they were chums. Shown her room and told by Margie with heated indignation the reason the two of them had been given the best, Marian said she couldn't be more pleased. She likes to be considered a woman, she said, who must be surrounded by luxury and loving care.

Our expedition on Monday was to Hampton Court. It was Whitmonday, the last day of the longest holiday on the English calendar, and everything in London consequently was closed. We decided it was a good time to go into the country. We found this was also a decision every British family in that part of the country had made. Almost every kind of conveyance, except perhaps an oxcart, was on the road, each of these spilling over with people. Therefore, our progress was not rapid but everyone was in high good humor. No one within our hearing fretted when the lines of traffic were halted for considerable periods. Instead, we all talked back and forth to one another across the lanes. Our driver was not the one we had had the day before. The name of this one

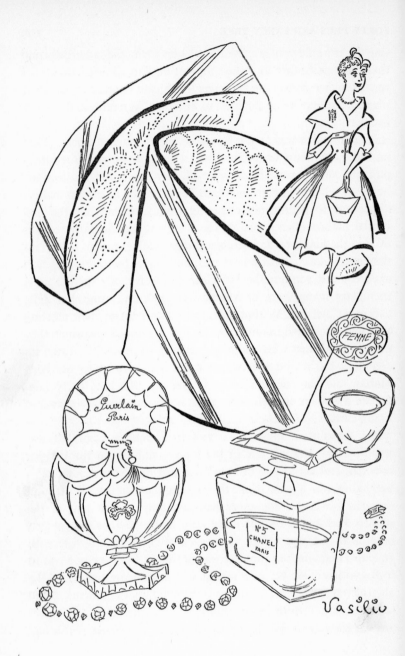

Guerlain
Paris

Nº 5
CHANEL
PARIS

FEMME

Vasiliu

was Clayton, he told us. We loved him from the start and from that day until I left for home he was my driver. The last time I saw him, he wished me Godspeed and waved me off when my plane left for New York. On the drive to Hampton Court I sat in front beside him. Now that we were five, there was of necessity an overflow from the back. Clayton is a magnificent driver, and praise from me is praise indeed because I am at most times in a car a craven loon, crying out wails of apprehensive cautions. Clayton never heard a wail. Clayton is furthermore a book of knowledge about England. He does not intrude this knowledge upon you but, if asked, can tell the identity of and something about anything that catches the eye. He is first in the lineup after the theater. He knows every short cut in London. He is always ahead of the time he was requested to come. And this in the morning, too, no matter how late he has been kept out the night before.

His full name is Arthur Clayton and he can be hired through Wimbush & Co. Ltd., Hyde Park Corner, London S.W. 1. Telephone: Sloane 0151.

There was, in the beginning, only one barrier to a beautiful communion between us, but happily this barrier melted away. The barrier was none of his building; it was my own ear, that sensitive, highly attuned instrument in which I had taken modest pride for many years until it dulled on me when the Italian language struck it. Now it dulled again, refusing entry to Clayton's speech. Clayton is a Cockney and his accent is pure and undefiled by any other neighborhood. Now I, born in the Middle West, have lived more years in the East than among my native fields and have in consequence acquired, my friends tell me, some Eastern overtones of accent. But Clayton has admitted no such diluting and on the way to Hampton Court I could understand scarcely one word he spoke.

No one was happy about this; my friends in the back seat insisted I repeat to them what he was telling of the things and places we passed. I thought it something less than polite to ask him to repeat a sentence the instant he said it. Prodded from the rear,

however, I did make this request again and again, and each time
he granted it with not a sign he found it tedious. It was with
the utmost politeness, after we had traveled an hour or so, that he
pointed to a billboard calling my attention to the advertisement
there. The product advertised was a hearing aid and the illustration was of a gentleman wearing one of these devices and announcing in a caption below that life was beautiful since he had discovered Little Wonder Worker.

"Do they 'ave those in h'America?" he asked me. "They tell me
it's a wonderful thing. Mikes your 'earing good as new, you might
say."

I considered this an epitome of tact and thoughtfulness.

The gardens of Hampton Court were a glory of color. We
walked along their paths, paused while I took a picture of wisteria
against the walls, then walked until we came to the maze. For old
sake's sake I entered it again, because once before, years ago, I had
got lost there. In the years between, I discovered, my wits have not
sharpened. I got lost again, and just as it had happened the first
time, was finally extricated by the gatekeeper.

The day had become unbearably hot and we had had enough of
walking. We returned to the car and went in it to the Mitre Inn
though it's only across the way from Hampton Court, but an English "way" can be long. The inn is attractive. It was crowded that
day and under such adversity I thought the service remarkably
quick. I cannot give the food there that much commendation,
though my palate may have been impaired by the tendency of my
tongue to cleave to the roof of my mouth. The reason for this was
that with every minute I became increasingly aware that at half-
past three in London I was going to do a broadcast to America.

My friends wanted to go home part way by boat, and have the
car pick us up at Richmond. I agreed it was a delightful idea, but
not for me. I wanted no possibility of being held up by crowded
river traffic. I preferred to leave my trust in Clayton where it was
already firmly placed. To my surprise they considered my point of

view reasonable and not fussy. It did not occur to me, and I never suspected until they told me later at home, they knew I was nervous about the broadcast. They decided, too, without my knowing it, that if I went back to London alone I would have time and opportunity to think out what I was going to say, and they felt that would be a good thing. What they told me was they yearned to go on the river and, if I didn't mind, they'd get themselves home.

I rode to London alone in the back of the car and with no word from Clayton. I think he reasoned that since I hadn't been able to hear what he said when I was sitting beside him, there was no use trying to communicate with me when I was removed to the distance of the back seat.

All the way back to town I thought about what I was going to say and consequently when we reached Broadcasting House I was awash with incoherence and confusion.

Peggy Broadhead of BBC, bless her, had been allotted to me as nurse-companion. I had waited only a minute in the lobby when she came running across it to welcome me, and introduce herself. She is young, gay, pretty, vivacious and very knowledgeable. She mothered me through corridors, downstairs, around corners and into a studio that had in it a chair, a table, and on the table a microphone. On my left, the wall of the studio was a plate-glass window that gave me view of the control room on the other side. It was just like the studio in which I worked in New York and, recognizing this, I began at once to feel a little at home.

Peggy left me seated at the table, and a moment later appeared on the other side of the window in the control room. A young woman was already there, working at an instrument panel, but I was astonished when Peggy, turning a switch so that we might communicate with each other, introduced her companion as the engineer who would control my program. Radio engineers in America are men, but in the ten broadcasts I gave from London, nine of the engineers running them were women.

When Peggy closed off the switch I did not feel so at home as I had felt a few moments before, because though I was not frightened now with the job immediately at hand, I was overwhelmed by a realization that sitting alone in this room I was, at a signal, going to crawl out through the microphone in front of me to America, and that in New York someone at CBS would answer me. I do not know why this is any more remarkable than communication by telephone across the ocean. But when from the other side of the glass the engineer dropped her arm, finger pointed at me, as a signal that the way was open and that I must send out my call, I felt the hair at the back of my head curl a little.

I think my voice was shaky when I leaned forward and said into the microphone, as I had been directed, "This is London calling. This is Emily Kimbrough in London calling CBS, New York. . . . This is Emily Kimbrough in London, BBC, calling CBS, New York."

And out of the microphone when I had said this, four, five, perhaps six times, came an American voice, strong and firm, "We hear you, Emily Kimbrough in London. This is CBS, New York. We hear you, Emily Kimbrough. Contact made. One minute, please."

And in far less time than that, almost instantly, out of the microphone came the voice of my radio partner, Harry Marble. "Hello, Emily," he said, "how are you?"

And we were on the air.

Chapter 18

LONDON WAS on tiptoe with excitement. The Coronation was only a week away. On the day after our Hampton Court jaunt, we made our first excursion about the city itself. On the afternoon before, Clayton had taken a course of back streets in order to deliver me without delay at Broadcasting House. Our route, added to my preoccupation, had made me unaware of the crowds that were in town. But Tuesday morning we drove down Bond Street, Regent Street and Piccadilly. The sidewalks were not broad enough to hold the number of people walking. Pedestrians strolled along beside the motors, and they in turn could move only in what I termed, because the over-all confusion was contagious, a "pail's snace." No one, afoot or in a car, was impatient; or if there were any restless ones we neither saw nor heard them. Those within our range talked happily, back and forth, exchanging news about what streets already had decorations installed.

Clayton told us he had learned at the garage that the like of the crowds in the city on Whitsunday and Whitmonday had never been seen. He explained that always before people had used the long week end as an opportunity to get into the country, but this time folk from all over England had come up to London instead, because they wouldn't be able to come on Coronation Day. They could at least see the decorations, though all of these weren't in place.

Every morning during the last week the crowds would discover a new section that had burst overnight into waving, floating garlands of color, and news of it would be called back and forth across the traffic everywhere. You couldn't always hear the hammering, but it went on all day and all night as workmen boarded up shop windows and set up stands in front of them. As these went up along the route, more and more people had to walk in the street, and that of course slowed traffic down even more until it moved at a very old snail's pace.

No matter how many times I called myself a sentimental old fool for such behavior, I seldom saw the decorations without a lump in my throat. This wasn't because the trimmings were so beautiful, though indeed they were beautiful. But there was a special quality about them. They weren't oversized, they weren't mechanical ingenuities that lit up suddenly or gave out sparks or counterfeited waterfalls, but they had been designed with imagination and taste, executed with fine craftsmanship. And by their very absence of gadgetry, they looked to me as if they might have been made at home by loving hands, and that made me swallow a little, like the old fool I'd said I was.

Consideration for people, too, had affected the patterns of the decorations. Those in places that might obstruct the view of watchers in stands or windows were made of a transparent material. And wherever garlands were strung across the street they were well above the eye level of any audience.

I do not know what artists designed the street decorations, but the name that people in the streets called across to one another, and that people everywhere talked about was Constance Spry. "Constance Spry planned the flower arrangements." "Constance Spry did the flowers, you know." "The flower settings are all by Constance Spry." Her name has been famous for years to everyone in this country, as well as England, who has grown or purchased flowers, because she is the greatest artist of all in flower arrangements. I myself had heretofore regarded her with a mixture of awe and resentment, and thought of her every time I have arranged flowers. When I arrange flowers invariably the arrangement, and the little holders on which I have spiked the blooms, fall forward into my face the instant I release my hand from them. But I shall never feel resentment again of Constance Spry, only awe.

Banks of flowers were at street corners, fountains, outlining some stands; assembled according to her diagrams, and they were masses of beauty that none of us who were in London during those days will ever forget. Americans will not forget either, I think, that for all the time they were in place, not one pot was taken by souvenir hunter or vandal, not even a blossom plucked.

We lunched at the Ritz. It was gay, crowded; the food delicious. That afternoon on the way to my broadcast Clayton and I held conversation. Overnight my ear blockage had cleared and I could understand him. Probably the number of other Cockney voices I had heard on the streets had broken through the sound barrier between us. But pulling away from the Ritz, he requested the doorman to ask me if I wished him to return from Broadcasting House to pick up my friends. I understood him. I answered immediately without the doorman's intermediation, and Clayton's involuntary start nearly took us up over the curb.

At the first opportunity he turned round and looked at me with a courteous manner, but with perplexity on his face. I think he was endeavoring to discover if I had somehow purchased a hearing aid and was wearing it. Some minutes later he observed he'd heard some people were quite affected in the ears—he pronounced it "h'ears"—by flying, and didn't get over it for several days. I knew then this was how he had resolved to his satisfaction the miracle of my recovery. From then on he pointed out famous clubs and other landmarks along our way and I was interested and grateful.

We arrived at Broadcasting House half an hour earlier than my scheduled time. One of the minor inconveniences of the traffic jams was that they made it impossible to gauge the allotment of time needed to go from one place to another. The only safe way was to figure exactly twice the time it would ordinarily take. You were safe then, but also, you were sometimes early. Still you didn't dare shave it any finer.

I sat in the car going over plans and a schedule for the remainder of the day. Leaving the car I told Clayton I would be gone long enough for him to get himself tea, if he wanted. He thanked me but said he preferred to wait, adding that he enjoyed the sight of the crowds. " 'Ave you noticed, Madame," he asked, " 'ow many h'Americans there are?"

I told him I hadn't.

Sometimes it was by their hats, he explained, or by their shoes. The obvious ways were the cameras they carried and the big pocketbooks the women had. "Never saw 'andbags that big," he added admiringly.

I indicated a couple on the sidewalk across the way. "I think I see what you mean," I said. "The lady hasn't a big pocketbook, but it is an American couple, isn't it?"

"Oh no, Madame," was Clayton's answer, "h'excuse me, but it isn't. That's h'English."

I wanted to know what made him so sure.

"Look at the way they're walking, Madame," he explained. " 'Er so h'independent, and 'im just h'ambling h'anyway 'e fancies, paying 'er no mind. If it was h'Americans, 'e'd 'ave 'is 'and under 'er h'elbow, and 'elpin' 'er up and down the curb, steering 'er, like. 'Arf carry their women, they do."

We had high tea at home and went to see Noel Coward's Quadrille, with the Lunts. Discussing it later at supper at the Hyde Park Hotel, we gave it unanimously high praise and bestowed also our approval on London's early theater hour, with dinner afterward.

The following days were busy and we were scattered. Once in a while in Italy I had been nagged by the candid question Margie had asked Sophy when our trip had not yet begun, "Do you know anyone in London?" Every time I'd thought of it I'd tried to conjure up at least one person I might find there and bring home to

dinner. This would scarcely count as the round of entertaining Sophy and I had pictured, but at least it wouldn't be so barren as Margie's prediction. Sophy and I had shared an uneasiness about the social scene ahead of us. It didn't occur to either of us in any of our speculations, what took us only two days in London to realize: that there were plenty of friends and potential guests in London, and that we hadn't time for any of them. There was too much to see, there were too many other things we wanted to do.

I was preoccupied with my broadcasts gathering up material and interviewing people for them. The five of us always met at the house for tea, but by mutual and clamorous insistence, there was a rule that if any one of us annexed a gent for tea—and we did achieve that much—she had first choice of drawing room or library. The rest of us took the room she didn't want. If both rooms were requested, gents taking priority over any other guests, the rest of us had tea in the apartment.

We went to the theater almost every night, but Thursday, May 28 and Friday, May 29, were the memorable ones. Neither of these found us in a theater. On Thursday we saw the Closing of the Tower of London. This is a ceremony anyone may witness by writing for permission to the Chief Warder's office. The Chief Warder is Mr. Arthur Cook, and we were the guests of Mrs. Cook. Peggy Broadhead at BBC had arranged this for us and I shall always be grateful to her.

We arrived at the outer gate around nine o'clock. We should have come earlier, but we had not realized there was so much Mrs. Cook had to show us. She took us first around the outside, and we paused, shuddering, at the Traitors' Gate and at the Bloody Tower. We climbed up and up circular stairs to the apartment of Mr. and Mrs. Cook, made from what had once been quarters for distinguished prisoners. The view from there is magnificent. It may not have seemed so to those prisoners, and the windows were not so wide then.

Mrs. Cook showed us her husband's dress uniforms. The one he would wear the following Tuesday in the Coronation procession was hung apart from the rest. Mrs. Cook said she brushed it and polished the buttons a little more each day.

About half-past nine she hurried us down the stairs again, and we took up our places where she indicated in the courtyard below. There were not many spectators besides ourselves. We learned from her that no more than fifty are permitted each evening.

A small company of Guards marched toward us from the inner part of the grounds and halted near us under the archway of the Bloody Tower. We heard the echo on the cobblestones of foot-steps in marching rhythm coming toward us from the direction of the outer gate. This was a company of Warders in their uniform of the Beef-Eaters, headed by Mr. Cook, and when it reached the company of the Guards, the Guard's Captain called out, "Halt! Who comes there?" The Guards halted.

The Chief Warder stepping forward answered, "The keys."

The Guard asked, "Whose keys?"

The Warder answered, "Elizabeth's keys."

The Captain of the Guards' response was, "Advance, Elizabeth's keys. All's well."

The Chief Warder took two steps forward, raised his Tudor bonnet and called loud, "God preserve Queen Elizabeth."

Guards and Warders answered in unison, "Amen."

And cued so perfectly with that word that they came on the instant, the clock in the tower sounded the first stroke of ten, and up high on the ramparts a bugler sounded the call, "The Last Post."

This is a ceremony that has been repeated every night for over seven hundred years, and we saw and heard it in moonlight.

On Friday night, May 29, Sophy and I went to a Coronation concert in St. James's Palace. The invitations had come to us through our friends Gina Bachauer, who was to be soloist, and her husband Alex Scherman, who was to conduct a small orches-tra. Mrs. Warren Hastings Pearl had arranged this benefit concert, and our invitations included a request that we be her guests afterward at a small supper party at Claridge's.

"You will wear your very best dresses, won't you, darling?" Gina had inquired anxiously over the telephone when the invitations had come.

We assured her such as they were they would be our very best.

I don't know whether Cameron or Clayton was the more pleased with us for garnering these invitations. Cameron not only pressed our dresses but dressed us in them and escorted us one at a time from the house to the car where Clayton stood, his uniform shining, his face beaming. From house door to car door, Cameron held my train, and from the chill draft that reached me, I think she must have held it extraordinarily high. Once she had settled it around me in the car, she returned for Sophy, and when we were both seated to her liking, she backed out, joined the other two maids who had come on the front steps, and all three of them waved us out of sight.

For the last two blocks of our way to the palace we were in a procession of cars bearing other guests and were back at the old snail's pace again. And again there were pedestrians walking along beside the cars. But these turned out not to be sight-seers of the Coronation trimmings. They had come out to see the guests going to a party at St. James's Palace. They were interested, and friendly. It was one of the most heartwarming experiences I have ever had to be visited by one after another of these onlookers. A smiling face would appear at the open window of our car and an admiring voice would say, "You look lovely, dears. 'Ave a good time, now do."

Immediately inside the palace is a large entrance hall, and at its far side a wide, winding stairway. Standing in the hall I heard a loud voice shouting from somewhere above stairs, but because of the murmur of voices in the press of people around me, I could not distinguish words in the shouting.

We moved up the steps slowly, completely hemmed in by other

guests, and I must have been halfway to the top when I recognized that the shouting was an announcement of the entrance of each guest. Now even in my world I have been announced at a party. But never, until that night, had I heard arrivals announced in such ringing tones and a volume that is used at parties at home when calling cars parked two meadows away. Neither had I, before this night, paid particular heed to my own name either by sound or classification.

But when above and ahead of me I heard roared out to the crowd the announcement of: "The Duke and Duchess of Something-or-Other," "His Excellency, the Spanish Ambassador," I felt my name was not for shouting.

I had had an experience something like this only once before, and waiting on the stairs I remembered it vividly. It had taken place on an occasion that in Hollywood is called a "premeer." When a picture is launched with this particular fanfare there are grandstands put up outside the theater and floodlights trained on the entrance, to catch and illumine the incoming guests. The grandstands are always filled and their occupants in a state of hysterical expectancy. Outposts take up their stand at the curb and as each car draws up they look inside, identify the occupant, and report at the top of their lungs that identity to the waiting crowd. "It's Ginger Rogers!" they say. And the crowd yells, "Yay, Ginger! Turn all the way around so we can see you." And Ginger obliges.

When I had attended one of these premières, an outpost had looked into my car, looked again, turned to the crowd and yelled, "It's nobody!"

At the top of the stairs in St. James's Palace, I mumbled, "Miss Emily Kimbrough," and as it was bawled out by the major-domo whose voice I had been hearing, and who I now know is called the toastmaster I muttered, "It's nobody," and scuttled down the receiving line, and who the ladies were who filled it I have not the slightest idea.

The throne room at St. James's Palace is exactly what a throne room ought to be, hung in deep rich red brocade, with a ceiling of carved ivory and gold, and a great crystal chandelier. On the walls are larger-than-life portraits of royalty done by Gainsborough, Sir Joshua Reynolds and the like, the chairs gold and upholstered with the red brocade that covers the walls.

Once settled in our places, Sophy and I relaxed and watched the rest of the audience filing in.

A nurse I once had for my children always used to say of something she admired prodigiously, "It's more than gorgeous." The men in the audience that night were "more than gorgeous" in their full evening clothes and their decorations, a wide red ribbon here and there across a chest, and sometimes a large jeweled insignia at the throat, tied around the neck with a red ribbon.

The women were almost all of them handsome, but not nearly all of them were smartly dressed. The clothes of many of them had seen long wear. They had a look of having been too often cleaned and pressed. But how superbly almost every English-woman carries herself. It gave me a twinge in my heart; they stood so straight, the dresses of some of them so out of style, and the jewels of nearly every one of them so magnificent.

I pointed some of these out to Sophy and whispered in her ear, "They'll do without new clothes or any other sort of luxury. They won't part with their jewelry because they consider it's only in their trust; they've got to hand it down to the next generation."

Sophy agreed, and we watched an elderly woman come in and find her place in the row ahead of ours. Her dress was gray chiffon; once it had been finely pleated, but the pleats had collapsed into dejected folds. She wore her white hair drawn up into a soft coil around the crown of her head, and she wore around her neck a necklace of large diamonds. A minute after she was seated, she stood up to arrange her coat over the back of her chair, and arranging it, faced us. We saw at the end of the chain of diamonds a pendant of emeralds and rubies that caused me to blink.

The members of the orchestra assembled on the dais in front of us at the end of the room. Alex Scherman made his entrance, rapped with his baton, and we all rose for the national anthem. They played only two bars of it and as I sat down again, I thought how sensible of them to render this token of homage, but not go through the whole of it. My dress was of black tulle with voluminous skirt and long train; it took a bit of arranging whenever I sat down. When I had completed this and gathered the separate folds over my lap so they would not be in the way of my neighbor, I looked up again ready for the concert to begin. I saw that everyone else was still standing. I dropped the folds and lurched to my feet in confusion. Everyone was looking toward the doorway through which we had all entered. I looked, too, and saw the major-domo who had announced us, step across the threshold and stop.

He put his head back and shouted, "Her Royal Highness, Princess Marie Louise."

As he bowed low, there came in so briskly it was almost a little jog trot, a small and very old lady. She went halfway across the width of the room, and as she passed them, the ladies in the front row curtsied, the gentlemen bowed low. She took her seat in the center of the front row in a special armchair. Her lady-in-waiting followed, and after dropping a curtsy, took her place beside the Princess. Mrs. Pearl, who was to be our hostess later in the evening came next, curtsied, and was seated on the other side of Her Highness.

The national anthem was then repeated and after that, as I took careful note, we all sat down.

I cannot count the number of times I have heard Mozart and Haydn played, but I don't think the count will ever go above one for hearing them played in the setting for which they were written, the throne room of a palace.

I did not see Her Highness during the intermission, but Sophy and I walked through the rooms that were open, and they were beautiful. We talked briefly with Gina and Alex, congratulating them on the wonderful music and arranged to meet them at Claridge's.

At supper I found I was seated three places away from Her Highness. Sophy was at the same table across from her. The Princess sat on the right of Mrs. Pearl. The party was in two private rooms and there were additional tables smaller than ours in each of these, perhaps sixty or seventy guests in all. Whenever I thought I wouldn't be noticed I peeked around my neighbors for a glimpse of royalty, and it delighted me to see that though physically she was very thin and slight, Princess Marie Louise was at the same time a stout trencherwoman.

We were served an elaborate supper and Her Highness engaged in very little conversation but concentrated on her food, course after course, eating every scrap on her plate. When she was presented with the menu and asked to select a sweet, she rejected all of them. They were not to her liking, she said, though she said it most courteously. And immediately after she had an idea that made her eyes twinkle as she expressed it. She had enjoyed very much, she said, the shrimps served as a first course. She would like instead of a sweet to have another dish of those shrimps.

I am a middle-aged sissy. I had taken only a bite or two of the shrimps that had been prepared with a heavy rich sauce. I had only nibbled at other food presented, and had allowed myself a few sips of champagne; this because I was tired, it was late, and I am not entirely confident of my digestion.

But at one o'clock in the morning, Her Highness the Princess Marie Louise, ate with gusto a five-course meal, substituting for the fifth, a second and ample round of the first. With the meal she drank champagne, fixing it exactly to her liking by producing from her evening bag a little gold swizzle stick.

I had opportunity to talk a little with her lady-in-waiting, Lady Hamilton, who was charming and spoke with affectionate candor. "She wears us all out," Lady Hamilton told me. "She is absolutely tireless, up at seven every morning, and she never goes to bed before one or two. We all adore her. At a party at the palace the other night, Her Majesty wanted to stop around half-past eleven, but Princess Marie Louise, her great-aunt, wouldn't hear of it. 'When I was your age,' she said, 'I would have kept the party going all night.'"

During the meal the major-domo, who had evidently accompanied Her Highness from the palace, stood behind her chair. When she had finished the last of her shrimps she said to Lady Hamilton she would like to say a few words. Lady Hamilton promptly turned round and communicated this to the major-domo, and he, stepping to the table and leaning forward between two guests, produced from his pocket a round object that looked like a small brass doorknob.

He pounded three times on the table with it, and said—and I had never heard before the phrase of classification—"My lords and ladies—ladies and gentlemen—Her Highness will speak."

Her Highness rose and made one of the most charming speeches I have ever heard, expressing, she said, for all of us our gratitude to the artists of the evening, to Mrs. Pearl for having arranged the concert, our appreciation of the music we had heard. She then paid tribute to Mrs. Pearl herself, wishing she said, to say aloud something of the warmth and affection she felt for her friend, our hostess.

I am sure her speech was spontaneous, but I have seldom heard better phrasing or more articulate expression of sentiment.

As we applauded it, Gina, from where she sat, leaned across to me and confided, "You know, she has such knowledge and appreciation of music, she is a delight to all musicians. And what a memory! When I come back from a tour she asks me to come and see her, and she always says things like, 'Now last season I remember you played such and such with Mitropoulos. What did you give him this year?'"

When the applause had subsided, Her Highness told Lady

Hamilton they must go now. Lady Hamilton indicated this to the major-domo; he rapped again with his doorknob on the table and announced, "Her Highness is leaving."

Immediately we all rose, the ladies she passed curtsied, the gentlemen bowed. When she had gone through the doorway, we sat down again. But I had no sooner settled my tulle around me when the major-domo was standing behind my chair.

"Miss Kimbrough?" he asked.

"Yes," I answered.

"Her Highness," he said, "would like you to come to be presented to her." He drew back my chair, I rose to my feet, and with that rising my lower limbs took on the consistency of Jello that hasn't set.

The last time I had curtsied was when I was at Miss Hinman's dancing class in Chicago and thirteen years old. "What if I step back into my train?" I thought wildly as I teetered toward the door. "I'll not only go over on the back of my head but I'll pull Her Highness down on top of me. This will make an international incident, and this is not the time for an international incident."

But something told me I could not say to the major-domo, "Ask Her Highness if we could make it some other day, when I will have had a little practice."

We had reached the other of the two rooms reserved for this party. The guests had risen from the tables there, and were standing in a wide circle around Her Highness, who, with her lady-in-waiting, was talking to Mrs. Pearl. The major-domo led me up to Mrs. Pearl.

Mrs. Pearl said, "Your Highness, may I present to you Miss Emily Kimbrough?"

Her Highness held out her hand. I took it and sank in a curtsy. I have never known what it was to have any trouble in my joints, but on that curtsy my left knee, bending, cracked with the sharp sound of a blown-up paper bag that is "popped," so loud Her High-

ness' hand in mine flinched, and I could feel Mrs. Pearl beside me
give a start.

I did not step on the back of my dress, however, nor did I pull
the Princess Marie Louise down. With the aid of a sudden sharp
pull from her hand, I rose again. But I think she found when I
had relinquished it, her palm was moist from contact with mine.

She knew something of what I had written and when she said
so, I felt myself blush with silly pleasure. She asked if I had come
to England to write a book, and when I told her I was there to
do broadcasts, she said quickly, "Now that's very interesting. I
should like to talk to you about that. Do you think you could
draw up a chair and we might sit down for a few minutes?"

The most mortifying phrases came instantly into my mind.
Things like, "Well, I guess we could," or "Why not?" But what
I managed to say aloud was that this would give me great pleasure.

The major-domo drew up a chair for each of us. We sat down.
Mrs. Pearl left us, the other guests went back to their places. But
in a minute or so Mrs. Pearl was back again and Sophy was walking beside her. Sophy has been blessed by nature with rosy cheeks.
At that moment, no one seeing them would have known it. Because of a deficiency of nature, Sophy also has to wear glasses. She
was not wearing them when she came to meet the Princess, and
when I saw her without them, I felt rising within me a tide of
hysteria I thought I would not have the power to suppress. I was
conjuring up, in a dreadful mixture of anxiety and malicious hope,
the possibility that Sophy without her glasses would not be able
to distinguish between me and the Princess. And if, confusing us,
she would grant to me a deep curtsy, I would hoot loudly and un-
controllably. I would not like to be asked in a game of "Truth"
whether I was pleased or disappointed that she did not confuse us.
I will admit, however, that I was not particularly pleased when she
made a low and graceful curtsy to the Princess without a sound.

The Princess asked if Sophy, too, could draw up a chair, and
when this was done, turned back to me and asked if I had read

what was currently being written about the Coronation, particularly had I seen the *Times* that morning?

I told her I had read it and had thought it admirable, and remembered that somewhere I had learned I must address Her Highness as "Ma'am" and I did.

She wanted to know then if either of us had seen *The Golden Book* and the book on the music of the Coronation.

We had not seen them.

Learning this, she interrupted quickly, "Oh dear," she said, "I should so like to give you myself a copy of each of these, but I do not believe that is possible, because, you see, these days they don't let me out."

She explained, "My schedule"—she pronounced it "shedule," of course—"is so full these days, with so many official visitors coming for the Coronation, that I am kept as rigidly to it as a schoolgirl. Now then," she went on, "I would advise you to go to the bookseller from whom I always get my books. He's just off the Mall"—pronounced "Mell," of course—"but poor soul," her eyes twinkled, "he's boarded up, too, just now."

She meant, of course, that grandstands had been put up in front of his shop.

She talked a minute or two about London at Coronation time, and then interrupting herself, turned back to me.

"I should like to say some things to you that I wish people in America might hear," she began "things about the Coronation perhaps they don't understand. I'm an old lady, you know. I'm eighty-five, and this will be the fourth coronation I've seen. So I know something about it."

She folded in her lap her thin, sharply veined hands, and looked beyond me as she talked, as if she were watching three coronations pass by.

What she said came back to me at the moment of the Coronation of Queen Elizabeth. I doubt that I shall ever forget it.

Chapter 19

ON THE morning of the Coronation I was in my grandstand seat at twenty minutes to six. After the long contest between Margie and Zella for the "kindness to others" medal, Zella achieved a final win on that day because she got up with me at four o'clock, made breakfast and packed sandwiches for me while I dressed. She and the other three did not have to be in their places until half-past seven.

Their seats were at Hyde Park corner, but BBC had secured one for me in a stand just outside the Abbey. All spectators in the stands around Parliament Square had to be in their places by six o'clock in order to clear the way for guests coming to the Abbey itself.

Everyone who sat by radio or television on June 2 knows that in England the weather was rainy, but only those who were there know how cold it was.

I left the house at five o'clock wearing my heaviest winter suit and thanking the Lord I had followed Barbara's advice and brought it with me. Under my suit I had on a sweater, and on top of it a heavy coat. I carried a raincoat over my arm because when I left the house the sky was overcast, though there were breaks in the clouds and it looked as if it might clear. To be on the safe side, however, I took the raincoat, and later on thanked Providence for this, too.

Clayton drove me by circuitous back ways and though there were cars and people along the roads we took, we were not caught in any traffic jam. We both knew, because we had seen them two days before, that spectators had set up camp on either side of the main roads the procession would follow. They had cooked their meals there on little spirit lamps, slept on the curb for two nights in the rain, wrapped in blankets, raincoats; some of them protected by pieces of tarpaulin stretched over their heads across sticks planted in the grass. Now they would be gathering up their possessions and moving into an orderly line under the direction of the police. Consequently, those streets would be impossible to travel.

Clayton was able to take me all the way to my own stand, but when we conferred with a bobby there, we knew it would be impossible for my car to return after the ceremony. The bobby anticipated this road would be blocked several hours then, fetching the guests from the Abbey, who in turn must wait until the procession had gone.

I had an imperative engagement. I must somehow be at Broadcasting House to go on the air to America at seven o'clock and tell what I had seen this day.

Accordingly, Clayton and I arranged to meet, when the procession should have passed, at the far side of Westminster Bridge.

An usher showed me to my place, and I settled in, tucking my accessories around me: box of sandwiches, Thermos of tea, camera, two books and the morning *Times*, these brought along as diversion from the tedium of a long wait ahead. I never opened one of them. There was no moment of tedium. I was in the third row, but the stand was not as yet filled. I walked down the aisle to the railing and leaned over it, since there was no one behind whose view I would obstruct. I was joined there a minute or two later by a delightful Englishwoman who entered at once into conversation. I would not have dreamed of making such an overture, and I am still surprised when the British do it, because I have not yet got used to the breakdown of British reticence that has occurred in recent years.

My companion told me her husband and children were parking the car. She had hurried on to make sure their seat reservations were in order. She was on the lookout, too, she confided, for a young nephew. She didn't suppose she would actually be able to pick him out in the crowd but hoped she might, and was a little anxious about his appearance.

"You see," she explained, "he's to be a page in the ceremony."

I found this exciting and told her so.

"Yes," she answered, "it's very nice, really. And of course he must be properly turned out. You see they live in the country. His parents are driving him up to town, and the only car they've got is an old station wagon. They always carry vegetables and animals and the children in the back, with hay on the floor to make it soft. So I do hope before he goes up the aisle, someone will make sure he hasn't any straw in his hair."

It was not a possibility I had associated with the crowning of a queen.

A company of soldiers swung into our square. My neighbor identified them. "Those are our cadets," she told me, "from Sandhurst."

As they passed immediately below us I estimated the average age must be a ripe seventeen. They lined up along the curb on either side of our street, and on an order from their commanding officer, who was perhaps an elderly twenty, came to a halt by means of three such violent stamps I should have thought their spines would be driven up through their skulls. I suggested the possibility to my neighbor, but she assured me this was a customary maneuver and had not over the long history of Sandhurst affected the intelligence quotient of its graduates.

Immediately our guards were placed, cars commenced to enter Parliament Square and pass below us. By leaning far over the rail we could see the occupants leaving their motors and being assisted

by liveried attendants to a canopied aisle from pavement to the
door proper. In the gap between door and canopy, we glimpsed
snatches of red velvet robes, evening dresses, coronets, or a little
tulle headdress. My interpreter beside me explained this headdress
had been designed and established by order of the Queen as headgear for ladies who did not rank a coronet.

Some of the cars were driven by chauffeurs, but not by any
means all of them. A good number—and most of these were little
motors—were driven by their owner, and at the entrance a lady
would descend and, following that, the car would move across the
square evidently to the parking space designated. In a minute or
two we would see the owner returning, striding back across the
square, his velvet robes looped over one arm, his coronet tucked
under the other.

A voice from a loudspeaker somewhere behind came on suddenly over the sounds from the traffic below and the conversation
around us. This was evidently the voice of an announcer allotted
to our own section, because it identified for us the occupants of
the cars as they passed below us.

As my companion and I had watched and talked, the stand behind us filled. We were not aware of it until their occupants requested us politely, to resume our seats in order not to obstruct
their view. We separated and I did not see her again.

Our seats were the conventional ones of any grandstand with
a cushion for each place but sitting still, in spite of the proximity
of the seatholder on either side, in front and in back of me, I was
very cold. I drank a little hot tea from my Thermos jug and
wrapped my raincoat around me like a steamer rug. I discovered
in one of its pockets an envelope that contained a pair of thin
slipover galoshes. I put these on and they did warm my feet and
ankles a little.

The people filling the stands came into the square on foot.
Mine, I think, at twenty minutes to six had been the last car admitted before those bringing the Abbey guests had started their

own procession. The arrivals on foot waved to spectators already in the stands and had considerable difficulty to reach their own seats because the sidewalks were filling with detachments of Boy Scouts and other organizations of young people who were to be permitted to stand there.

A sudden roar drowned out the voice of our announcer. It came from the seatholders in the stands across the way from me, that bore across the front of one the name Canada, and the adjoining one Pakistan. It came from every stand around the square because the people in all of them had recognized without being told that Sir Winston Churchill was arriving at the Abbey door. They gave him a spontaneous salute with all the power of their lungs.

Not long after his arrival a voice that was not the one we had come to recognize as our own announcer's came over the loudspeaker. "May I have your attention, please?" it said. "This is a general announcement. Will all householders who are leaving their homes today please be sure their pets are safely inside and off the streets? And will all those driving in from the country make sure their domestic animals are being properly fed and watered? However, should an accident befall there are mobile units for animal care traveling within a radius of fifty miles of the city. One of these may be reached by ringing up [a number was given] and should be at your service within half an hour. One other notice, if you please, and this is very important. Do not light your bonfires tonight until you have ascertained there are no birds' nests in them."

The British, I said to myself, thought of everything when they planned this Coronation.

The line of cars to the Abbey thinned and then stopped. The last car arrived, the guests were assembled. The Royal Family came. The Horse Guards riding into the square heralded the approach of the Queen herself, and we caught a brief glimpse of her as she entered the Abbey.

When she had disappeared, we settled back in our stands to

listen, not to watch. Presently over the loudspeaker we heard the music from the choir and the opening of the ceremony. We heard the boys of Westminster stop abruptly in their stately, swelling anthem and shout in the shrill treble of schoolboys: "Vivat Regina Elizabetha, Vivat, Vivat, Vivat!" They cried it three times. It is the right and privilege of Westminster boys to be the first to hail the Queen and by this announce to the rest her presence among them. They resumed the anthem, and we knew Elizabeth was moving up the aisle.

We heard the Archbishop of Canterbury speak, and the Dean of Westminster, and all those others pledging their fealty, just as everyone the world over beside a radio or television that day heard the ceremony.

But when the moment of crowning came I saw and heard something that was not recorded on the air, but is recorded in my memory for all the rest of my life.

Our announcer said, "The Archbishop of Canterbury is holding the Crown above her head. He is lowering the Crown. He places it. Elizabeth is a Queen."

And simultaneously, without a word, but with a sound like a breeze through a field of corn, every person in every stand as far as my eye could stretch around Parliament Square, rose to his feet. I have been in an audience when a distinguished person has entered, and I have seen a little group of people rise to pay homage, and then another group, taking that as cue, follow, until the whole group has stood. But I have never before seen a spontaneous rising of thousands of people as I saw that day. Nor do I know why I rose. But I think I would have done it had I been alone. And that is what happened to all of us.

We stood in silence, and after the rush of sound as we got to our feet, it was very still. So that when they came, we heard them very clear: the Royal Artillery guns across the river first, then far off the 62 gun salute from the Tower of London to the new Queen.

And, standing there, I remembered the words of Princess Marie

Louise, daughter of Alexandra and Edward, sister of George V, Aunt of George VI, and Great Aunt of Queen Elizabeth; Princess Marie Louise, who was seeing at that moment her fourth Coronation. This is what she had said to me.

"Tell them," she had said, "that of course there is pageantry and there is pomp and splendor and rich trappings. But all those things make up only a frame, and in the center of that frame is one individual, who is given in turn symbols of the obligations of a monarch; the Orb, the Scepter, the Armils and so on. The monarch only touches each of these. They are not possessed by that individual. They are only recognized as responsibilities to be assumed. And when each one of these has been recognized it is returned to the place from which it came, and that is the altar. When this has been done the sovereign, all trappings removed, dressed only in a white, homespun shift, advances alone. I venture to say that in all the world at that instant, our sovereign is its humblest inhabitant. He goes to the altar having delivered up to it all the symbols of authority or power, and at the end offers himself to a lifetime," and she turned to me, "not a term of office, mark you, but a lifetime, of devotion, obedience and service.

"We're a funny little island, Miss Kimbrough, but those are the things we live by. Will you tell them this, in America, for me?"

"Yes, Ma'am," I'd said, "I will."

Restaurants

(European Trip—1953)

PARIS
Quasi modo—delightful, wonderful food
Café Lippi (opposite Deux Magots and more fun.)
Le Bollé—Place Michelin—a cellar, old, dark, fascinating

VENICE
Quadri in St. Mark's Square—excellent food, quite expensive
Harry's Bar for American drinks
Danieli Restaurant on the roof—delicious food, crowded, quite
  expensive
Risttorante Del Angelo—for lunch, just off St. Mark's Square—
  good food and inexpensive

MILAN
Drinks at Biffi's Café in Victor Emmanuel Arcade by all means
Dinner at Biffi's Restaurant—good
Palace Hotel Restaurant—food and service only fair

LAKE COMO
Villa d'Este—delicious lunch on terrace overlooking lake

ROME
Capriccio Restaurant—good food, not expensive—crowded and
  fashionable for lunch, not too crowded for dinner—a few blocks
  from Eden Hotel

Passetto—first-class, delicious food, expensive

Eden Hotel dining room—used only when no time to go out

Tre Scalini—smart restaurant—out of doors—delightful

Alfredo's—in Trastaveri—very simple outdoor restaurant opposite
   Church of Trastaveri—old part of Rome. Evening clothes make
   you conspicuous

NARNI

En route from Rome to Perugia

Albergo Bella Visto—wonderful bread, cheese and wine at little
   table in a window overlooking the mountains beyond

PERUGIA

Brufani Hotel—very good

ASSISI

Windsor Hotel—very good restaurant, but we should have gone
   to top of hill to Cafe D'Italia

FLORENCE

Grand Hotel—good food

Excelsior Hotel—cocktails and dinner excellent—more sophisti-
   cated than Grand

Doney's Café—for drinks before lunch—very fashionable

Doney's Restaurant—across the street for glorious food

Da Zi Rosa—near Grand Hotel—not fashionable but food and
   music wonderful

SIENA

Hotel Excelsior—very good

LONDON

The Hyde Park Hotel—good.

Ritz Restaurant and the Ritz Grill—excellent

Barclay—Claridge—Savoy Hotel—excellent

Queen's Restaurant, Sloane Square—inexpensive, delicious food,
   combination of smart people and old residents of the vicinity

Set in Linotype Electra
Format by Katharine Sitterly
Manufactured by The Haddon Craftsmen, Inc.
Published by HARPER & BROTHERS, New York

Paris

ROMA

VENEZZIA

MILANO

ASSISI

Sienna

EUROPE

Firenze

LONDON